CANON
FODDER

POEMS INSPIRED BY
CLASSIC LITERATURE

PRAISE FOR *CANON FODDER*:

"In an age when most poetry collections are quiet affairs, slender in size and modest in ambition, Jay Sizemore's **Canon Fodder** swims through the ocean of contemporary poetry like Moby Dick, huge and unstoppable. Sizemore is to poetry what Jack Kerouac is to fiction, a passionate, funny, deeply human voice trying to catch the whole world in words." — George Bilgere, author of *Blood Pages*

"Never trust a poet who has no interest in reading great literature, which, as Dr. Johnson teaches us, is a kind of intellectual light, like the light of the sun that enables us to see. Jay Sizemore is that rare breed of poet who sees clearly and sings beautifully. And he writes with more honesty and erudition than anyone I've read in a long time."
— Norman Minnick, author of *Advice for a Young Poet*

"If you love writing and great literature, you've got to read Jay Sizemore's *Canon Fodder: Poems Inspired by Classic Literature*. He writes like nobody else.

Sizemore writes and comments beautifully and evocatively about: the nature of the self, the hunger of the dying, the fate and impermanence of art, the world we live in with its mass Walmart shootings and its funerals, and its joyful dancings and yearnings.

My first creative writing teacher told me the best response to a piece of writing is another piece of writing. Jay Sizemore has learned that lesson better than anyone I've read in a decade. Read *Canon Fodder*, and then you need to go back to the writers you love and do what Jay teaches here: Write that poem about the work that touched you most. Write that and write another and another and never stop."
—John Guzlowski, author of *Suitcase Charlie*

CANON FODDER

JAY SIZEMORE

Crow Hollow Books

Also by Jay Sizemore

Father Figures: autobiographical poems
Confessions of a Porn Addict
SCOWL: Revolution Poems
The Ghosts of Silence
Fukushima Franco: the social media poems
Pariah
life:death:love:theft
eulogy/elegy
white/guilt
Mein Drumpf: poems to make America great
Second Amendment Pastoral
American Love Poem
grief
All the Light in the Wild Blue Sky
thieves
Corona: pandemic poems
Censored (out of print)

It's Not All Bad : short stories

Published by Crow Hollow Books
Portland, Oregon

Manufactured print on demand

10 9 8 7 6 5 4 3 2 1
ISBN 9798767352470

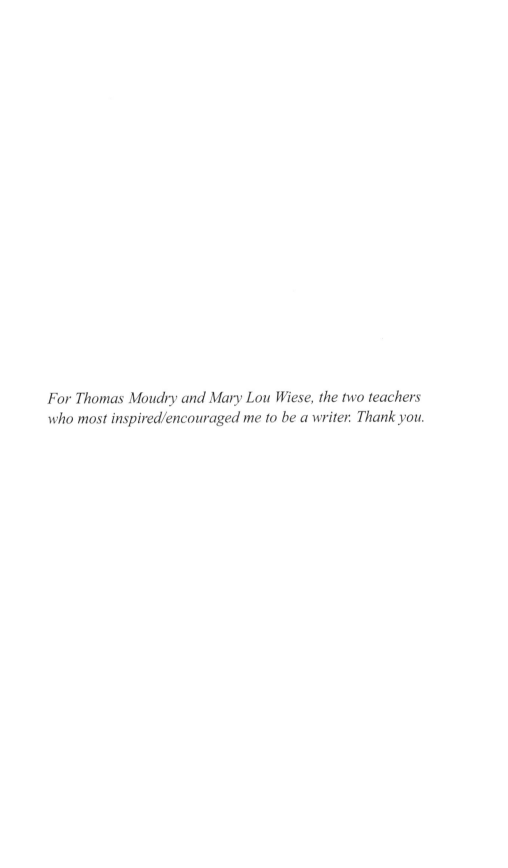

For Thomas Moudry and Mary Lou Wiese, the two teachers who most inspired/encouraged me to be a writer. Thank you.

TABLE OF CONTENTS

For first you write a sentence, And then you chop it small;
Then mix the bits and sort them out Just as they chance to
fall: The order of the phrases makes no difference at all.

~Lewis Carroll

FORWARD: A Note on CANON FODDER

Everyone has those books that they've always wanted to read, but they just never managed to find the time. For me, that book was *Moby-Dick*. I had picked that one up on many occasions, telling myself I had to do it. It was important. I love the first chapter. Love it. I consider it one of the best opening chapters ever written. I've read that chapter four or five times, but every time I started this novel, considered one of the greatest of all classics, I would find myself bogged down by the density of the prose, and eventually just abandon it for something else.

Some might say this is a flaw in the work. But not really, it's just a difference of perspective, how attention spans have changed over the years. I knew the writing was excellent, and the story was epic. Clearly it has remained admired for all these years for multiple reasons, being a powerful story of monomaniacal obsession and revenge, and written in a lavish and stylishly evocative prose. I'm just a shitty reader, with the modern attention span of a gnat.

Then, in early 2020, around May I believe, I had an epiphany that changed the way I managed my time and reading habits dramatically. In my career path, I work at a job that allows me a lot of down time. Basically for much of my day, I am walking around, waiting for something to happen, being in the security business. As you can imagine, this waiting can be monotonous and often abysmally boring. The mind wanders. It gets creative with its ideas. This can be productive for a writer, or it can be degenerative, allowing the muscle of the brain to weaken, like an unused bicep.

In 2020 though, I had begun filling some of this monotony with music, and some podcasts, just filler material to occupy my thoughts with something other than my own voice. Then, I realized, I could be spending this time listening to audio books! I did, after all, have the Audible app on my phone, an app I hadn't used in forever, when several years ago I had listened to a few books during long commutes. I thought to myself, hell, my entire day is basically one long commute.

And thus I began down a path that would become a sort of obsession, and one that I would find more rewarding than I ever possibly imagined.

The first book I tackled this way was *Moby-Dick*. I said to myself, no excuses this time. It's do or die. Finish this motherfucker, or be damned.

I'm not going to lie, it was still challenging. But it was hardly impossible. It took me about a month, but I got through the book. I'm not entirely positive that all the chapters about all the varying types of whales are essential to the narrative of this story, but somehow I managed to get through them without killing myself. The rest of the book I found to be utterly amazing and compelling. Easy to see why it has stood the test of time.

The best part of this process for me though? While listening to the novel, I found myself enthralled and inspired by the style of the writing. The word use. The sounds of the sentences, how they rolled like poetry. How certain phrases stood out like powerful monoliths of language in the mind. I found myself compelled to write some of them down, to turn them into something else, something of my own.

The best writing often does this to me, as it should to any creative person. The best work inspires others. This is not the first time Moby-Dick had inspired me. I had already written a poem that was inspired from the first chapter of the book, which I wrote the very first time I had tried to read it.

This time, I wrote a poem based on a reading of the entire novel. While I shamelessly borrowed from Melville quite a few turns of phrase that burned incandescently in my brain, and some key vocabulary choices, I twisted these into a poem that felt like a jigsaw puzzle forming images and statements of my own making. I found that the poem I made from this process ended up being one of the favorite things I had ever written. That poem, and few others written this way from other novels, was later published with *Terror House Magazine*.

I consider the process I used in writing these poems to be a version of hybrid erasure, where I borrow one of two phrases from the novel (sometimes more, sometimes less), a few vocabulary words that really stand out to me, and then I fill in the gaps with my own inspiration, be it the overall emotion that this novel is pulling from me, the overall themes of the work, or whatever it is causing me to think about at the time. The process was so inspiring, I decided to roll with it. I had not really been writing a lot, and this seemed like a great way to get my juices flowing.

Some might question the ethics of this, or consider this method a form of plagiarism, but it's definitely not. There's a long history of authors using similar methods to create new work, be it in "found poetry" or "black out" poetry, or even "cut and paste" poetry. Burroughs famously cut and pasted lines from other sources to create many of his works. As far as my process goes, the source artist is always credited, and I do not rely so heavily on their material that it removes my own voice, or my own creativity from the final product.

I'm paying homage to the source author, trying to be guided by their voice, while connecting the dots of inspiration to find something new to say. Call it a "pin the tail on the donkey" process of writing a poem. For the most part, the bits of phrases I am borrowing from the source text are so blended with my own words, it would be challenging for readers to isolate and discern the exact moments in every poem that were the inspiration. It's my hope that this leads people back to the source novels that I read for each poem, and it leads people to read them either again, or for the first time, and that it can inspire more people to engage with the work with new eyes.

Next, I read *The Grapes of Wrath*. This one was another novel that I had wanted to read for long as I could remember, having loved *Of Mice and Men* for ages, but I had just never found the time to try it. I've been kicking myself over and over for avoiding it ever since. The book is absurdly powerful, and prescient about the nature of capitalism, and the human instinct to manipulate the system for personal gain. I was floored by it. Certain passages felt prophetic, downright harrowing in their insight. Steinbeck was a certified genius.

Again, I was inspired to write a poem. Again, the poem seemed to me to be one of the better things I had ever written, albeit more vaguely tapping into the root themes of the novel. I said to myself, hey, if I keep this up, I could really put together quite a collection of poems. This began the snowball rolling down the mountain.

The third novel I read/listened to was *Blood Meridian* by Cormac McCarthy. Brutal and brilliant. From there I started tackling works that seemed daunting in their breadth and had a reputation for being difficult reads.

First, I worked my way through *Infinite Jest*, one that notoriously I had heard many say they abandoned without finishing. Next, I would set my sights on *Ulysses*, but taking a break between them with the Faulkner novel *As I Lay Dying*. All of these produced poems from me, some of them multiple times. And in the process I was getting acquainted with works that were renowned as foundational to literature.

While I can't say I really enjoyed *Ulysses* much, it was still rewarding, and at least I know what all the fuss is about around it now. To me, Joyce seemed rabidly anti-Semitic throughout that book, with only one passage toward the end that attempts weakly to walk back this rhetoric, and I found that a bit troublesome for a novel that is so highly esteemed in the canon. I didn't dwell on it, just an observation.

As I worked through these classic novels, it became a challenge for me. How many could I get through in a year? Could I get through a majority of what many considered "The Top 100 Novels of All Time"? Utilizing such lists, I added works to my queue that I intended to read. I asked people to suggest great books to me that I may have not heard about, and added them to my growing list. I decided I would focus on attempting to read one major work from each author, and write one poem inspired from their work, trying to get a good variety of represented authors in my budding poetry collection. It started coming together gradually, and added up quickly to a substantial amount of new work.

Some of these poems were published with other journals like *ImpSpired*, and more recently with *Punk Noir Magazine*. One of them was accepted to The *Dead Mule of Southern Literature*. I was happy to find that I wasn't the only one believing these new poems had any value.

The process has continued through 2021, and including several poetry collections that I've read and other additional stuff, I have managed to read 68 books for the year as of August 21. Now, I am hoping to get through 100 books by the end of the calendar year, setting this lofty goal for myself while understanding that it is very attainable at my current rate of reading.

Spending these past two years studying and absorbing such highly regarded canonical novels, and more modern masterpieces, I have found myself endlessly thankful that I have taken the time to do this. It has been such a rewarding and life-changing experience to engage with much of this work. And it has been enlightening to see how so many common threads weave their way through this material over such an extended period of time.

Authors are often directly in communication with their predecessors in many ways, having either been influenced by them, or linking their work together through allusion and commonality of theme. It seems almost like a chain of creativity, linked down through the centuries, with the ghosts of authors linking hands with authors and pulling this giant concept of art into the future. It truly boggles the mind to think about it.

So many of these books will stay with me the rest of my life. So many of these characters will live in my heart forever. If I'd never started this project, I would've never discovered how much I loved *Anna Karenina*. How perfect the novels *Ethan Frome* or *Animal Farm* are, in their genius and craft. That my favorite book of all time was written by a philosopher! It's impossible to put into words how much this journey has changed my life, my perspective, my appreciation for what it means to be alive.

Below is a complete list of works I've read since I started this project:

2020:

11/22/63 by Stephen King
Cat's Cradle by Vonnegut
Don Quixote by Cervantes
Infinite Jest by DFW
Blood Meridian by Cormac McCarthy
Moby Dick by Herman Melville
1984 by Orwell
Ulysses by James Joyce
The Grapes of Wrath by Steinbeck
The Sun Also Rises by Hemingway
Rant by Chuck Palahniuk
Ham on Rye by Bukowski
Post Office by Bukowski
As I Lay Dying by Faulkner
Damned by Chuck Palahniuk
The Largesse of the Sea Maiden by Denis Johnson

2021:

Jimmy & Rita by Kim Addonizio
Crime and Punishment by Dostoyevsky
Metamorphosis by Kafka
Brave New World by Huxley
Red Rover Red Rover by Bob Hicok
Factotum by Buk
The Sound and The Fury by Faulkner
Animal Farm by Orwell
The Hellbound Heart by Clive Barker
Tale of Two Cities by Dickens
On the Road, by Jack Kerouac
Little Boy by Lawrence Ferlinghetti
Strange Case of Dr. Jekyl and Mr. Hyde by Robert Louis
Stevenson
Coney Island of the mind by Lawrence Ferlinghetti
The Bell Jar by Sylvia Plath

Lolita by Vladimir Nabokov
How to Write One Song by Jeff Tweedy
Poetry as Insurgent Art by Ferlinghetti
Lisey's Story by Stephen King
Frankenstein by Mary Shelley
The Invisible Man by H. G. Wells
The Witchcraft of Salem Village by Shirley Jackson
Connecticut Yankee in King Arthur's Court by Twain
Anna Karenina by Tolstoy
I only came here for the music by Mary Wiese
Now We're Getting Somewhere by Kim Addonizio
Pride and Prejudice by Jane Austen
Rusty Stars by Linnet Phoenix
Wuthering Heights by Emily Bronte
100 Years of Solitude by Gabriel Garcia Marquez
Jane Eyre by Charlotte Bronte
Gravity's Rainbow by Thomas Pynchon
My Man Jeeves by P. G. Wodehouse
The Soft Machine by William Burroughs
Breakfast at Tiffany's by Truman Capote
Thus Spoke Zarathustra by Friedrich Nietzsche
Tropic of Cancer by Henry Miller
Song of Solomon by Toni Morrison
Hunger by Knut Hamsun
Steppenwolf by Hermann Hesse
The Picture of Dorian Gray by Oscar Wilde
Treasure Island by Robert Louis Stevenson
Pale Fire by Vladimir Nabokov
Madame Bovary by Gustave Flaubert
Lunch Poems by Frank O'hara
To the Lighthouse by Virginia Woolf
American Pastoral by Philip Roth
Rhythm and Mucous by Mather Schneider
Flowers of Evil by Charles Baudelaire
Essays by Ralph Waldo Emerson
Swann's Way by Marcel Proust
Ethan Frome by Edith Wharton

A Sleeper's Truth by Mather Schneider
Tender is the Night by F. Scott Fitzgerald
The Rainbow by D. H. Lawrence
Heart of Darkness by Joseph Conrad
Far From the Madding Crowd by Thomas Hardy
The Trouble With Being Born by E.M. Cioran
Gulliver's Travels by Jonathan Swift
A Room With a View by E. M. Forster
Henderson the Rain King by Saul Bellow
For Whom the Bell Tolls by Hemingway
Fuck It by Leia John
Journey to the End of the Night by Louis-Ferdinand Celine
Conversations with Professor Y by Celine
Alice's Adventures in Wonderland by Lewis Carroll
Through the Looking Glass by Lewis Carroll
Underworld by Don DeLillo

-Jay Sizemore, August 22, 2021

Part One

A WRITER DREAMS OF AMERICA

~after Jack Kerouac

A dust cloud hangs
over the American West
like a benzedrine dream,
pornographic pictures and
power lines, a madness
that burns phosphorescent
plume and fume,
yellow as the noon.

The mad gather
like clotting blood,
like spiders made of stars,
glowing neon filament fibers
stringing web between the dark
and the moon, drawing gazes,
dropped drooling jaws.
This is what we want.

The specter of Karl Marx
in the wings
of a flaming magpie.
The dueling desire
of a typewriter and a parachute,
a speeding bit of shrapnel
tearing through the spleen,
the American Dream
gone miniature
as a rocking chair
viewed through a telescope
held backwards to the eye.

I

This is the writing life,
the romanticized road
stretching from ink to page
and lip to stage,
a kind of ubiquitous rage
that releases itself like rain.
We're all hitchhikers or bums,
traversing the wild country
in the back seats
of jalopies, dinosaurs knitted together
from strange bloody rust,
and the views from these windows
are what memories are made of.

In Anytown, Anywhere
the rivers run raw and fragrant,
a murmuration of wet
rippling against the quiet
subconscious of the mind,
that mildew scent
of wet earth and birds,
where experience bends
to meet expectation
like a wet kiss
upon the forehead.

I find myself here so often,
searching for my identity
amid so many names
scrawled messily on the wall
of some flop house
or abandoned railroad car,
and I feel just as lost

as a journalist's hat
blown beneath the bleachers
of a retired baseball stadium
where yesterday missed its handshake
with the normalcy of today,
and my mouth waters
for the familiarity
of apple pie and ice cream.

I miss that spirit,
the spirit of the West
slouching like a cowboy
on a bar stool
sipping his beer,
this mud dappled stranger
with carnivals for eyes
and a smile whiskey warm,
asking if anyone needs a ride,
because there's always
some ghost worth chasing
out past the pines
and the hills and the night,
where such kindness
feels welcome as a puppy
licking the salt
from the palm of your hand,

these visions are vanishing
like flickering phantoms of light
after all the eyelids
have closed their carnivals down,
there will be another huckster
in another huckster town,
saying step right up,

step right up and test your luck
guessing the weight
of a million empty years.

ADDIE BUNDREN SPEAKS TO AMERICA

~after William Faulkner

A word is just a shape the mouth makes
to fill the void of not making it,
as America is just the name
of earth and water preparing
to be nameless as the dark
and the bloodless bone
absent of all tongues,
all memories, all men
good for nothin' but hate.

America does not know it is dead.
I lay in the dark and I listen
to it breathe, this land that is now
my blood and my flesh,
I listen to it weep
not knowing that I hear it weeping,
the shapes of my words
seeping like molasses from my pores
and swirling back towards their births,
an idea of time reversed

making me a fish
slippery and slick,
flipping free of a child's hands
back to the river,
to the river black as blood
which is my blood
and which is your blood
and the blood of the yet unborn.

I am dead as America is dead,
and neither of us are ready
to admit we are ghosts
wandering a graveyard, searching
for the mother we never had,
our mouths unable
to manifest consonants or vowels,
to create the shapes of sounds,
yet wet with the ache
for milk not tasted.

The Art of Hearing/Healing

~after Friedrich Nietzsche

I.
Life itself is involuntary,
to exist within
the song of the night,
was never a choice,

but the repercussions
of myriad choices believed
stealing dominoes
from the fingers of silence,

choices that themselves
were not choices
but mere instincts
of beings

convincing themselves
they were free
to be anything
other than animals.

II.
For the last time
have I spoken to the dead,
what good is happiness
where the rope dancers fall?

What good is a God
oblivious to the art
of dance? Sleep is more
precious to thieves

than the promise
of heaven. This body
is the creator of dreams,
of evil, of parables

with grasshopper legs.
This body is capable
of teaching gods to waltz,
of love's greatest fatality.

This body is the cage
that invented cages,
that put itself on stilts
and declared itself a mountain.

These hands are eulogies
and death is a festival
in praise of lost virtues,
castles trapped in the ether

where vengeance is a tarantula
poisoning the conceits
of justice. The state is a liar,
a hospital for bad poets,

mirrors swallowing mirrors
reflecting the sun
reflected in sea,
a resurrection requiring a grave.

III.
There are no gods
capable of cleansing this body
with dirty water or words,
or teaching a body

to subsist merely on praise.
There are no gods
preventing time
from devouring his children,

calming the waves,
clearing the ears to hear
what the body refuses,
the eyes to see

the absence of what never lived,
the serpent that speaks
from the stem of the apple.
There are no gods tuning violins

alone in the woods, asking the body
to love this solitude,
beyond the fear of lonesome
death, the insistence of fangs.

There are no gods asking
for abandonment of reward,
allowing death to simply be
its own attainment of release.

There are no gods admitting
their ignorance
of what this all could mean,
allowing that creation could be

itself a kind of vanity,
when dogs believe in ghosts,
but there are no gods
listening to mongrels,

or canines gnawing bones
along the streets of heaven,

there are only poets whispering
and ignored in the gutters.

THE ART OF UGLINESS

~*after Louis-Ferdinand Celine*

Could I be the last coward on Earth?
The years stretch out like
the most seductive of lies,
with the night more inviting
than death, that black asshole
waiting.

Horses are smarter than men
in that they don't carry
a righteous belief in war,
nor go chasing clouds
like rolling reams
of living velvet.

I've been hornswaggled
over and over
by such notions of celebrity
and the immortality of words,
the violent cumulative disharmony
found in self-worship
and desires kept warm
by the thought
of a stranger's adoration.

The medium of the universe
is eternity, and so
I am a pimp for eternity,
careening through life
on this vessel
harboring its wealth
of bellicose and phantasmagorical passengers,
each obsessed
with their own egress.

You end up feverish,
asleep in a cove of tinnitus,
the termites of the wind
devouring that fragile edifice
segregating self from selfless
and dream from dreamless,
drunk on quinine and wine
beneath that yellow
mosquito net sky,
eventually just begging
to be allowed to die.

THE BEANSTALK TO THE DARK SIDE OF THE MOON

~ after Toni Morrison

The dark has many colors,
variations as splendid and mysterious
as the many minds that hold it,
this definition of blackness,
of midnight, of the new moon.
It may as well be a rainbow,
this thing people fear.

America is a good garden
for guns and grave diggers,
things that sprout
like dull and colorless tulips
from soil that never birthed
anything other than blood.

America is just a water mark
left on a mahogany desk
in the vague shape of a tooth,
something that aches
and whispers *freedom*
beside an inkwell,

a slave holder scribbling
We The People
upon a yellow scrap of parchment,
words barely visible
by candle light.

America is the dream
of owning things,
even people,
especially people,

most of all.

Within this dream your mother cries,
and instead of tears
black petals drop
from her eyes
before splashing like oil
in a blue wash basin
shaped into a star.

America is the vulture
that sees itself in the mirror
and finds a peacock
in full plumage display.
She's the carnivorous giant
tumbling from the clouds
even as she believes
she's always been Jack
with his pockets full
of magic beans.

Watch out, she's in your ear,
and right now she's trying
to convince you
there's no such thing as color,
and the only way to escape
the heavy yoke of the past,
to slip those shackles and bonds,
is to forge a new set
made of sweat and gold
and don't forget to smile
while you wear them.

THE BIRTH OF POLITICS

~after Mary Shelley

The elixir of life is a chimera,
such ardent pursuits of lightning
reflected in metaphysical forms
dark and cleaved
as a philosopher's stone.

This is discovery,
nature of the unnatural
ardently unearthed like veins
hidden beneath the faces
of foes fixed in fervent frames.

Banish every idea of pedantry,
embrace the ardor
of an arduous mind, fixated
on the secrets all scientists
must struggle upstream to find.

Knowledge is dangerous,
to drive nature from its hiding places,
to animate this lifeless clay,
to give birth to thought, that blue worm
within the broken brain of decay.

I am the unhallowed wreck
of my own obsession,
anxiety made manifest
by the lunar delights
of cadavers rewired

nerve by meticulous nerve,
I am the creator of madness,
psychopathy bestowed through
such ardent and pure intent,
the garments of ghouls unkempt

must loose their graven soils
from their folds. Red blood darkens
like the eyes of men
who've forfeit their souls
for the gold and idols

their would-be fame enthrones.
Both God and man
cast their shadow upon the stage
neither alive nor aware
their dark ardor is one and same.

BIRTH OF THE BODY

~after James Joyce

All homes eventually become pawn shops.
You become the ghost of your own father,
a dead treasure of hollowed bones—
click clack clackety
dream catcher of decay.

The sea hides its faces,
sun flung spangles, dancing coins
on the surface of the water—
Form of forms,
Body of my body,
Mind of my mind,
Shell of my shell.

Lamp light and wormwood,
Ouroboros
of laughing corpses
and the secrets of stone.

Man becomes God becomes man
becomes sea becomes seam
and stars and skeletal chasms
of the sky of the earth,
under swept and scuttled
a capsized ship
speaking to the lapping waves.

Corpus Christi with a tree frog
rescued from a sink drain,
opera music swelling

as it leaps from my fingers
to the damp foliage,
body glistening
a pulsing river of green.

I am the tree frog.
I am the foliage.
I am the hand,
and the promise of teeth
beyond the pines.

There is no main character here,
no protagonist except time
and breath, the incessance
of sound that lives
with or without being heard.

On Charles Bukowski's 100th Birthday

Charles Bukowski is not 100 years old
because Charles Bukowski
is dead.

The bluebird in his heart,
once famous
for its persistent attempts
to escape, to fly, to sing,
is now just as dead and decayed
as old Buk in his casket.
A different kind of cage.

Charles Bukowski is dead
and he doesn't care
about your distaste for the canon,
politics, or pronouns.

He'd say, better to have another drink
than worry
what other people think
about what other people think.

He'd say, what the fuck is a facebook?
The critics always wanted
a place to loiter
and listen to the sound
of their own voice,
without hearing the voices
of the crowd,
the muted applause
of back patting
like the thrum of a murderous hive.

Charles Bukowski would laugh
at the thought of a Twitter Mob,
an entire horde of bluebirds
polluting art
with their maddening chirps,
cold and heartless.

He'd say, leave me alone. I'm dead.
I haven't had sex in 25 years.
I haven't tasted whiskey,
haven't felt the burn
of tobacco on my tongue,
haven't groped wildly
from my bed
in search of that shadow
always threatening to strangle
the life out of me.

I'm Charles Bukowski!
I'm not a fucking symbol
for freedom.

Somewhere, the sound
of a whiskered chin
scratched,
smoke drifting hazy
before dark brown eyes,
searching for that next
impossible line,
a ghost in a wooden chair
alone at the library.

Charles Bukowski is dead,

and you best get used to it,
to the idea
that one day
you too will join him
in the ground.

He'll meet you there.
He'll smile.
He'll say, happy birthday.
How many poems
did you carve into the sky?

THE BUSINESS OF LOVE

~after D. H. Lawrence

You can't hitch your horse
to the shadow of a fence post,
the heart tugs at the reins
of such fecund darkness,
a bull rushing
among the bulrushes.

The clanging torment
of passion is a fire eater,
a millstone rolling,
heavy sky upon the earth
pressing down, relentless
in its gravity, its need.

What am I but fruit
to be crushed
and fermented for wine,
a body meant for drinking
and exhilarating the senses
until repetition numbs the nerves,

leaves the tongue lonely
in its bicuspid cage,
wanting for the taste
of something new,
a mouthful of salty pennies
pulled from a fish's stomach,

or a tangerine
soaked in tequila sunrise.
Love flashes bright,
like a punch to the nose,
but then it fades

to a dull ache
just before it's gone.

You can spend so many years
trying to duplicate it,
that first blush,
the first crimson drunkenness
of a heart's hymen torn,
but you always end up
just waiting to be born.

WHAT IS ALL THIS IF NOT CHEMISTRY ATTEMPTING TO EXPLAIN LONELINESS

~after Gustave Flaubert

The science of the heart
is a most medieval medicine,

a bloodletting meant
to be the cure for boredom,

where marriage acts
like a lancet, spraying scarlet

explosions of color
upon a white porcelain bowl.

It's best to amputate the hand
that reaches for the magic

mirror of another,
their face aglow with ardor,

a false idol, false comfort
that lures like the light

of an angler fish
dangled luminously above

its snaggle-jawed maw.
This is the promise of love,

which fades like the grasshopper's call
across the meadow in the dusk,

horizon a balustrade of embers
before lavender sheets,

wainscot clouds, colors that brim
with vertigo lust, but none of them stay.

One may as well choose a wave
cresting within the swell of the tide

and promise to follow it
until it breaks the illusion of time.

DANCING LESSONS FROM GOD

~after Kurt Vonnegut

If I wanted to end the world,
they'd give me the Nobel Prize
for perfecting genocide,
for understanding the plight
of the garden plow
and inventing the first religion
to call prayer nothing
but a poem in excrement.

The cat's cradle
of God's love
can be found
in the indices
of the unholy.

But what is God?
What is love?

Time, such a beguiling bastion
of the illusive spirit,
its passage like a staircase
accepting the momentary weight
of our countless footsteps,
where we fool ourselves
into believing we matter
more than we are matter.

The ragged rim of oblivion,
welcoming as a leper's smile,
calls us from our oubliette

to explore,
to build the better bicycle
and pretend
not to feel the cold
of the nuclear winter,

where the snow falls
like orange blossoms,
and the horizon yawns,
a Calypso
made of beautiful worms.

DEAD POETS DON'T BITE

~after Robert Louis Stevenson

A poet is just a pirate
with a belly full of rum,
ready to set sail
across uncharted seas.

His arabesque is loaded
with black blood for ink,
his cutlass is sharpened
on the unimaginable brink

of an abyss that stares back
with a malevolent wink.
For it hides in its bosom
quatrains a poet seeks,

perfect stanzas, perfect rhymes
worth more than gold,
these are the treasures
for which these lives are sold

like cheap secrets
told to loose parrot tongues,
mutiny burns colder
than the strongest of rums,

these poets, these cutthroats,
stay willing to stab holes
through the hulls of their mothers'
boats, for nuggets of truth

they forfeit all claim to souls.
It's why they're drunk to the gills,
singing shanties and songs,

this lust for words kills,

dulls all sense of moral dread,
for these poems live on
long after their poets are dead.

DEATH CAN'T GROW A MUSTACHE

~after P. G. Wodehouse

You can't rattle Death.
He's not that sort of chap.
Death is the eternal optimist,
never worried if he will earn
credit or commission.
Death is an expert ornithologist,
but in his heart he's an artist
who prefers his practical jokes
to come before his breakfast.
Death would rather die
than see you adorned
in the audacity of chartreuse.
He'd rather you didn't
leave the house dressed like a circus.
People in pink ties
are not to be trusted
and neither are their ghosts.
Death is busy writing a travelogue.
He knows all the best restaurants,
all the best drinks, the best places
to sit and sip a coffee
amid the choral clamor of the crowd.
Death is the entrepreneur of want.
He's the only one with the power
to tell the crickets to *shush,*
shush it up right now, wot.
He's a friend to the animals,
and yes, even humans are animals,
though often drunk and horny animals.
Death is the only friend
who will never abandon you.
He's a poet for worms,
and a philosopher for birds.

Death loves a good game
of dominoes after dinner.
Jolly ho, by jove, pipped and bucked,
the good old chappy
knows everything about waiting,
and just what to do
about the bottom of the glass
and the bottle.
He doesn't give one fig
about your blue eyed boy,
but I'll bet you didn't know
how Death prefers his poems
read in English accents.
Try this one again, with rot.

AMERICA AS DON QUIXOTE ON ELECTION DAY

Polish thy armor and prepare
for a return to the age of chivalry!
Wear your gold washbasin with pride
and cast your stone against the tide!

For these are not stones, but birds,
birds that carry our voices
like ravens never to be killed.
A call and response, a cathedral choir.

When you address me, call me sire.
For my heart belongs to tomorrow,
where my lance has struck its home,
and vanquished the threat against all hope.

I vote, against the giants,
I vote, against the magics
that would turn brothers into enemies,
that would burn libraries

instead of lighting beacons.
That would build walls
between our hands.
This is my land,

where every house is a castle,
and every broom another sword,
to defend thy honor and nobility
from those who would steal,

and use the Other like a cudgel.
Arise, and be knighted,

the whole world is our table round,
we must slay the dragon

that with one exhale
could tear everything down.

SOME THOUGHTS WHILE DROWNING

~after James Joyce

It was a nun, they say,
invented barbed wire.
Hear the ruin of all space
engulfed in a match head's flame,
along with the beaches
and their white buoys
like fence posts tethered
to the darkness,
keeping nothing at bay.

Lodged in a library
of infinite words
your ghost might bray,
Render unto Caesar
the blood of the Ubermensch!

Does the quick brown fox
still leap
the untamable tides
of time?

After all,
God is just a child
shouting in the street,
Euthanasia or
a youth in Asia?

The metempsychosis
of a dog,
babe of a demagogue,

the mercurial crown
of myriad brutalities
ineluctable.

Drowning is supposed to be
the most peaceful of deaths,
a life revisited
in blinking phosphorescent
spasms,
a face washed pale
and drifting
among the languid
waving weeds, olive green.

I am unafraid.

The old gray fox
still sleeps in the shade
of the mildewed turtle's shell.

DUALITIES

~after Charles Dickens

The sea does what it likes
and what it likes is destruction,

a funeral for candles
buried in graves of deep mahogany

reflective flames floating
in leaves chocolate brown.

I exist as an automaton
I vanish into wisps of the will,

an emotionless machine
a conflagration of human hearts,

I'm the pock marked runnels in an ocean wave,
the myriad guttered rivulets

within the fractured glacial face.
I am the multitudinous diamond planes

predicting futures for triangular light,
I am the alpha and omega for footfalls

and every thought in between.
I'm you, I'm me, and I'm you and me.

Fate spins its pirouettes
like unread pages lost from the table

blown into dust devil spirals
of paper cuts and martyrdom,

I'm writing this directly on your brain,
and now your left eye itches,

as my right eye twitches
and we both sneeze,

two ghosts or one ghost or no ghost
reflected candles of

a funeral chandelier
shining on the jewelry of strangers.

DULCINEA DISENCHANTED

~apologies to Cervantes, for my friend George Love

On my deathbed, she came to me,
Dulcinea del Toboso,
peasant girl made maiden fair,
after I'd given up my armor,
convinced my madness
invented her beauty
like pale feathered swans
conjured from the thinnest of air.

On the sixth day she strode
into my room
as if gliding on currents
of indescribable clouds,
and she cupped my weakening heart
within her pallid, angelic palms,
whispering to me,

Not yet. Not yet, Sir Don Quixote,
your madness is but a blessing
and the world beats
within the chambers
of your self-made mythology.

Let me love you now
as you've always desired to be,
let us live among the sheep herds
and the hillocks of green,
I am here, your promise kept
your obligation fulfilled.

And I surveyed the moment
for any sign of malignancy,
my friends surrounded
and waiting,
Sancho Panza for once bereft
of proverbs,
as the priest seemed bereft
of prayer or psalm,

and I felt my strength
like a sudden wind
return,
as I spoke up, my words
brimming with hopeful resolve,

Oh, Dulcinea, my sweet sweet dream
at last made manifest,
it would be my greatest honor
to live and to love thee,
for to stay here
and partake of such treasures
would be the greatest
of all my Earthly
and misbegotten adventures.

And so Don Quixote, Knight of the Lions,
lifted from his slumber,
and lived happily
the rest of his peace-filled days.

THE ETERNAL FLAME

~after Charlotte Bronte

Tell the fire not to burn,
the disconsolate moan of the wind
hints at the birthplace of words.

A candlelight spell of warmth
meant to obviate caprice
away from childish contentedness
to a caustic churlishness,
pulling the yarn smiles
from the fabric faces of dolls.

The heart is an orphanage.
A fortress of whale bone and iron.
A slatternly cage of rotted boards and bars.
A storybook with all illustrations removed.
A garden blighted by bugs.
A skeleton made to dance and puppet emotion.
A chastity belt worn about the mouth.

When I was young, all the secret rooms
were red, and red was the color
of reading at dusk, light
like a convalescing balm
filtered through fluttering shrouds
of azalea blooms and leaves.

I told the fire to burn,
but to burn softly, gently,
the low embers of morning.
Amid the fragrant smoke

I waited for words
to form like beads
of melting frost
upon my tongue.

Language lives, enigmatic
and elusive as a sphinx,
a coquettish interlocutor
with a brocaded flesh.
Language, is a fortune teller,
reading a hand without lines,
a mist magnifying the moon.

I dare not feign
an air of superiority to doves,
love stalks my spine
like the padded paws of a cat,
while I sponge blood from a wound,
remembering claws.

Meet me alone in the gloaming,
dark rose petals dropping
from the sun,
the sky a blossom blanched
criss crossing garland of cloud.

EXCAVATING THE SELF

~after Philip Roth

I. Guess Who

Getting it wrong is living,
a misunderstanding
of the other, never knowing
the inner curves of the spiral
becoming the most human
of myriad human flaws,
perception itself a limitation.

An artist is a biography
of perpetual motion
capturing itself over and over
like a blood sample
squeezed beneath a slide,
lighted and dyed,
something frozen
that upon examination still moves.

An artist is a tanner at the tannery,
sewing together stretches
upon gruesome stretches
of his own harvested hide,
a patchwork of scar tissue
and faded tattoos
asking you to get warm
with the idea of sacrifice,
to feel beautiful
within something ugly,
to feel alive
within the clothing of decay.

The future is androgynous,

a crack that forms
before the cleaving,
something that was always
fractured beneath the appearance
of faces like stone,
a wink in the falsity of forever.

Time, that irascible river
that floods all houses
poised upon its banks
without the slightest of provocation,
moving the inhabitants around the board,
not like game pieces,
but granules of dirt
clinging to those pieces
while thinking themselves
irreducible to the outcome.

You wake up one morning,
and most of your friends
never knew you,
even as they're trying to remember
your awkward mannerisms
at the reunion
before you arrive
wearing the mask that time bestowed.

Wasn't it always like this?
A wasting of seconds and hours
playing *Guess Who?* with a deck
missing most of its matches.
A competitive circle jerk
where the prize
at the end of the climax
has always been a coffin?

None of us are ever as alone

as the exam table
would convince,
with its cold steel
and fragrance of antiseptic
mingled with powder and latex.

Even the doctor
must some day remove
his stethoscope
in order to hear the call
of his own heart beating slow.
But before then,
he says, *Deep breath. In.*

II. Surface Level

Does anyone know anyone?
Does anyone know themselves,
that beneath the layers
of somnambulance and sex
lives a monk in mid self-immolation?

You think you know your home,
the house you grew up in,
can still feel the polyester fibers
of its ugly green carpet
tickling your shins and your fingers
as you raced Hotwheels cars
along its ridges and grooves,

you can still smell it,
the sun-warmed ambience,
something like linseed oil
and vinyl, the gas flame
ticking to life in the stove,

the blanket you pulled
up over your nose
when at night, strange lights
flickered in the windows
from machinery working
its foreign and alien work.

But did you ever have cause
to look beyond its walls,
past its paneling and paint,
too see the guts, and wires,
its pressure-treated spine?
Do you know jack shit
about plumbing, electrical code,
or even how to read a level,
the different intonation
of a nail's hammered depth?

Have you been in the musky dark
of its crawlspace,
pulling spider web
from your face and your mouth,
cursing small rocks
hidden beneath the plastic
and how they bruised your knees?

Have you wondered
who lived there before,
or who might later
scratch with their thumbnail
at the hash marks
measuring your height
that your mother carved
into a doorframe with a kitchen knife?

Have you wanted to visit that place again,
only to find nothing

but a charred foundation,
some piles of ash
and a few blackened beams,
leaving you as hollow
as an ancient barn
that used to house tobacco,
but now holds only rats and owls
while it waits to collapse,

wondering if even your memory
of what you thought you knew,
bears any resemblance
to what actually was.

III. The Inner Heart

All this positive energy
cannot remake the troubled world,
when our secret inner lives
thrive on brokenness.

The sad inventory of domesticity
sounds like a knife sharpener
dragged across a blade
until that noise eclipses

the inner monologue of regret.
Everyone thinks about fucking
someone they should not be fucking.
Maybe this is an instinctual way

of coping with the unknowable,
how to prevent the mistakes
made by our children,
how to still feel beautiful

in such a pornographic age.
Our capacity for suffering
flexes like an infant's bones,
and adjusts within a bouquet

of blood-bloomed bruises.
Every parent is a house
slated for demolition
by the hands of the next generation,

where the art of sewing
the tight inner seams of gloves
has vanished into code,
and no one is sifting the rubble,

or willing to pay the ransom
of kisses that sealed
the pages of a scrapbook
tossed into six million flames.

FIESTA CORRIDA

~after Ernest Hemingway

Every day it's the running of the bulls
and every day it's a fiesta,
alternating sips of absinthe,
brandy, and beer,
tastes of licorice, caramel, and malt,
our bodies just gaseous
place holders for want
for something else,
something beyond these moments.

Let's go to Paris,
let's go to Madrid, to every land
in between, where the world
trundles forward
like a train on a track without end
and the people act unaware
of even being onboard,

where the sky opens itself
like the bare back of a bather,
where the mountains and the clouds
rest beyond the horizon
like crumpled butcher's paper,
and everything just lives
for the sake of living,

never minding the hearts
nor their desires unrequited
their ventricles filled
with cherry-scented smoke,

the mornings will be cold
as the afternoons will be hot,
the beaches bright and reflective
beneath an unforgiving sun,
which only makes the water
more appealing to the flesh.

FOR LAWRENCE FERLINGHETTI

I've never been to Coney Island,
I've never been to L.A.,
but I know these places all the same,
their ephemeral visages and skylines,
their storybook stories of love, of injustice,
of adventure like a ferris wheel
careening down a city street to the sea,
all its lights flickering and shooting sparks.

I've seen the wind act like a whiffle bat
smacking its ball, the sun,
back and forth across the sky,
with the moon dodging this play
by erasing itself slowly as a quarter
taking thirty days to disappear
when flipped from a magician's hand.

Sure, I've wanted to be a firefly,
a poet, a saboteur of ugliness,
but I've long been a refugee,
an escape artist constantly
breaking the surface of the water
after escaping the safe
he had promised the crowd
he could drown in.

But see, it's all performance
and subterfuge, a game of words
and music and pretend,
where we ask ourselves silent
as huddled charliechaplin men,
I don't know, man, is poetry
even relevant? Again?

Look at all those stars,

if you can still see them through the smog.
And if you can't, I promise
they're still back there, beating
their seemingly forever beats,
luring madness from the pores of the night.
And that is the kind of beauty
that leans out and over
the guard rails of the soul,
whispering some faint promise of purpose.

No one is born a poet.
The words build up
through rainstorms drumming
their beatitudes within
the great dark vault of the heart,
and only the lucky or the damned
who spend their lives chipping
away at the wall of that dam,
ever break through it,
releasing that flood of pent up
agonies, observances, soliloquies
sealed up in metrical screams
or unbridled dreams gone mad,
and isn't it beautiful
that all this chaotic energy
gets born through breath?

You tell me, is that madness,
or is poetry just the river
of the world,
and we are the light
kissed by its waters,
knowing that neither
was never meant
to be contained.

THE HELL SCAR

~*after Sylvia Plath*

My madness is mercurial.
I can prove it.

The floor will soon be littered
with glittery thermometer shards,
as I gather those silvery globs
like liquid mirror balls,
cumulative and amorphous,
balanced on the palms of my hands.

These poisonous shapes
are my pets now.

I'll soon absorb them,
soak them up
right through my cadaver skin,
the old fag of my heart
burning, *God damn, God damn, God damn.*

The problem with me
is how I desire to be everything.

And this is what it means
to embody inadequacy,
to become a stillborn
salvaged from the silver tray
and kept like an heirloom,
a dead baby in a jar.

The most beautiful thing on Earth

is an unblemished darkness.

We spend these lives
oblivious to the sour air
of our coffins,
corpses living inside of corpses,
so many bad suits
worn like the absence of sleep.

And then one day you wake up
unaware of how you escaped
the tornado unscathed.

HERMAN MELVILLE WRESTLES WITH WHITE FRAGILITY VIA MOBY-DICK

The sea is an asylum
vast and shoreless,
awash with the inscrutable
tides of god, a bilious deity.

Perdition's flame:
the low laughter
in latent horrors of life,
white curdling cream of the squall,
so ignoble a leviathan.

First draft of my final will and testament,
an elongated siamese ligature
dooms both poet and witness
to a tomb of whiteness.

Hunger: that incurable disease,
such a bleakened beatitude
like black stones cast amongst the shoals.

A dead and bloated whale,
flagpole stuffed into its spout hole

in teeth, in stars,
a jackknife.

They lie ensconced beyond
such mortal sights
where Death hides
in prairie-like placidity.

Dogs have more humanity,
mystical lung-sailed honeycomb,
my Queequeg, my savior.

The sea is our greatest murderer,
a riderless steed gone mad
and gnashing, bashing at skulls,
exposing the vestiges of bone.

The sea, the mirror of god and man
disentangles from the azure
an undulating apparition of life,
a ghost shaped like an ankh,
lost in the murky ink of the squid,
the white squid.

The profundity of the dark
steals many a harpoon
on some strange apostolic whim,

prodigious, prodigious, prodigious:
a rudderless skiff:
angels are sharks well-governed,
maggots in a wheel of cheese

a foamy confusion of entrails,
pantheistic vitality
sealed within the bowels
of whale men, of white men,
brows troubled with the morning.

Avast, avast, avast:
a serpentine winding
of rope and hook and wild,

like peeling an orange,
skinning the corpse
of the bounty.

Every manifesto begins,
writ upon the blank white sea,
a draft of a draft of a draft.
Call me Ishmael,
call me vagabond,
call me the great white whale
of the past
wrapped like a cadaver
in the whiteness of the sails.

You'll read this poem
through an isinglass,
an immense copper calm
unfolding like the mouth
of a bloom,
a bloom of beauty
that means to swallow
all syllables
from the language
of the sky.

HOW LOVE PERSISTS

~after Emily Bronte

Weather is the interpreter
of language before words,
where love is the querulous Pharisee
swallowing his carving knife.

I'm drinking to his hearty damnation.
My blood is a hell of tumult,
throwing this confession to the kennels,
I forgive my murderer.

One tree may grow crooked as the next,
no way to predict the knotted curl and twist
of limbs withering toward light.
Easier to spit out the taste of mulled wine.

The past is a winsome stone
the wind shall cleanse of dates and names.
Listen, beneath the quivering shade
amid such quiet earth and graves

there can still be heard
the ghosts of lovers quarreling.

AN INCONGRUITY

~after Virginia Woolf

Inspiration's vein
runs thin as a palette knife
cutting the shadow of a river
into a wet landscape,
nothing finished, nothing formed.

Shadows are the children
of the light, each absence
a hollow like a cavern
carved into the moon,
all a part of the sky
as individual waves
together form the sea.

And yet, people only remember
the brightest spots
on the horizon,
the sun god,
the lunar mistress,
the reflection of a wasp
hovering above a teaspoon,
white sails caught among the storm.

Such ghosts stalk the fringes
of the periphery,
background characters
in an impressionist work,
just smudges and swirls
blending as a backdrop of colors,

dark circles for mouths,
yawning as if in expectant awe
for that moment

when the undulating eye
of the lighthouse
might illuminate their being.

THE KNIVES OF THE SEASONS

~after Thomas Pynchon

I.
Your sound will be the sizzling night,
a contrail crystallized
like frost on a champagne glass,
smell of banana in the air.

You are a palimpsest of secret flesh
giddy with grandeur, *Achtung Baby!*
screaming across the sky,
a dust mote caught between

the gleaming buttresses of light
smoking through packs
of Unlucky Strikes.
Kindness is a ship of fools

springing leaks, and they stick
their fingers in until
they're paralyzed by fate.
You wish to write your name

upon every noiseless cylinder
expecting the infinite silence
behind Death's sudden smile,
you are a junk drawer

filled with rusty nails, corkscrews,
and unimaginable doom.
Teasing apart the concentric knot
of life and the anxiety of not life,

you are a surfer of slime trails,
a Zeppelin caught in a fly trap,
a dollar bill smeared in shit
and still used to pay down a debt.

Your mother is the war.
The city is Death's talc-white etching,
statisticians all striving
to become less than zero, metaphysical

imaginary numbers knitting together
the webbing of quantum space
and this thing we call the universe
or even reality, the tactile sensation

of fingers flipping pages
through ancient manuscripts
or the first owner's manual
to the world, wafting scents

of decayed flesh, those tiny organisms
that die between the bindings
of their bountiful feasts,
just like everything addicted

to dopamine and oxytocin, ether
and thrill-sought fear.
You are a puzzle of chromosomes,
of pimples, lust and experimental math,

fucking away the days
until all your semen stains
fade like an alkaline odor,

nights in the oyster bar

lost to the taste of horseradish
and light beer. You are an ocean
accepting endless debris,
the detritus of fallen satellites and rockets

clumsily missing their targets
due to the errors of human decimals,
quadratic equations solved for x
instead of y. You are the prism,

but you wasted so much of your time
believing yourself the rainbow.

II.
I am related by blood to the sea.
It asks me, *what are you doing tonight,*
my dark, secret child?
Buzzed by bombs, and the shuddering wood
of doorways filled with the visage of Death,
I ask the sea, *How much longer?*

Find me dozing along the gold-fringed
corridors of consciousness,
a space monkey oblivious
to his martyrdom, just happy
for once to feel weightless and floating,
a ghost caught in the viscous
fluid of the eye.

Life is Pavlovian by nature,

this flight or fuck response
to the presence of artificial thunder,
God's hand reaching through the clouds
to touch my throbbing erection.
I want to procreate
with the phalanx, producing a future
without arclight in the windows.

The air seems an oblique, luminous gel,
making the world a slo-mo snow globe.
I am not the protagonist,
not even in my own perceptions,
put your attentions on the flocks
of indigo flowers flourishing
within the craters of the blast sites,
their petals a burnishment of the wind.

III.
This is not a poem for children.
We are all lamps burning tonight
in precambrian exaltation.

We sit in evensong
of counterfeit babies,
lip rings, and sexual innuendos

meant in praise of the Holy Trinity:
profit, cancer, and global climate change.
We are all sufferers here

of acid reflux, dysphagia, sleep paralysis
a shadow's leash cinched
around the larynx. We wake up

coughing blood into our pillows.
We've seen the pathology

of reciprocal narcissism,

the monster fellating the monster,
a snow angel made by a grenade,
a dog with a needle in its brain.

Turbulence is in the ether,
a somatic disturbance not unlike entropy,
a surprise alignment of coordinates

targeting the location of doubt
within the power of the State.
History is an aggregate of finality,

martyrs dying with scents
of their own seared flesh
clinging to their nostrils.

IV.
Your head is a balloon hooked
to a helium tank. Your brain

is a frozen plum, activating
the salivary glands

in the mouth of William Carlos Williams.
You are your mother's teeth

grinding in her sleep, your sleep.
The cold scar of the moon

rests like a blemish on a pane
of opaque glass, and you are

the opaque glass, never the moon.
You are the pornography of blueprints.

You are so far away, no one can reach you,
not even I can reach you.

You are a V that stands for Victory,
not the V that stands for hippie Peace.

You are vertigo within the pain
of poetry, a dominatrix dipped in piss

forcing all supplicants to swallow
or choke on the contents of your shit.

V.
The bristle cones have outraced death
for a millennia. Gray light and rain drops
perspiring from the windshields
of automobiles afraid of intersections.
Mommy's little helper has never been confused
for an allusion to the Elves and the Shoemaker.
She died smoking an exploding cigar.
Our gravestones stand as monoliths
to the societies of the fire ants.
One must meditate for a lifetime
to stop the mind from searching
for the purpose of living,
never promised and never given.
The wheels of war roll on
like vertebrae shadows
and someone's writing a limerick
to commemorate the ashes
of six million un-thirsty skulls.
It isn't funny and no one is laughing.
Why must Victory subsist
on the melting of atomic bones?
Listen to the data. The great hum

of the zero sum. Go back far enough
and everyone is related... to fish.
The moon is the zero at the edge
of the world, the egg balanced
on top of a watermelon seed.
How many ways to describe
the same sky? Ask the madman
munching a tulip bulb in the corner.
This whole life is an experiment,
a conditioning maze meant to hide
the temporal loop of the race,
God's smirking face in the firmament.
A huge tungsten piano left standing
in a city leveled by collisions of hydrogen.
Memory is a Mandela Effect,
a moth with a million wings
changing the past to fit the mold
of a honey pot labeled Berenstain,
not Berenstein. You should learn
to love the bomb, to stop worrying
about what's beyond your control,
the world is a stomach sleeper
to keep itself from snoring,
and you never bothered to get the results
of your test for sleep apnea.

VI.
The meaning of life
sits on the edge of a knife,
You wish it were sharper
but your heart is a doctor
drilling lobotomies for his wife.

VII.
Let's go live

near the dust bowl seas
of the moon.

What is light, but the expression
of basic human hope,
every star an acupuncture point
in the body of God,
needles like lightning rods
threaded through with static
and cloud suturing this wound
of our longing.

The great crab in the sky
clacks its claws
and scuttles sidelong
through the ichor of the night,
imaginary, yet held
like a pillbug
in the jar of the mind,
still smelling of shine.

O Prometheus,
lend your flame to the wick
of this cocktail,
and grant some meaning
to this flammable hell,
this shell of tomorrow
inhabited by the most unworthy
of temporary thoughts.

If existence is believed a bulb
then life is the filament
flared to phosphorescent glow,
burning in the lamp
set upon the desk
next to the window
staring out into the void

like some yellow eye,

except it's not an eye,
it's a hollow cut into stone,
illuminated, yet empty,
just a small part
of a more elaborate structure,
a spinning windmill,
one blade tattered by joust,
something that lives
only in the imaginations of the mad.

Intermission

THE MAGA-MORPHOSIS

As Greg Stillson awoke one morning from frightful dreams, he found himself transformed in his bed into a Trump supporter.

The usual hangover headache of drowsiness and fog, his pre-coffee brain was gone, replaced now with a crystalline certainty about the world. Where previously much had been shrouded in mystery and doubt, now, he felt only a morose calmness. He knew the grand conspiracy of deep state design. He knew vaccines were evil instruments of the Devil. He knew global climate change was a hoax. And most importantly, he knew Donald Trump was sent by God to lead his chosen people. Within his newfound calm, there was a purpose to his life that had never been there before. It was invigorating. He felt he could do anything. That every answer about the world and existence was a mere youtube search away.

Then he remembered that he still had to report to work for the Amazon warehouse by two, and suddenly he hated his job more than he ever had.

Lying in the bed, Greg felt encumbered with extra weight that at first seemed to come from nowhere. His breath came in ragged gasps. He looked himself over in wonder. Overnight it would seem he had gained somewhere in the neighborhood of two hundred pounds. He now wore a shirt that only featured a large letter "Q" on it, which barely wanted to cover his midriff, rising up to expose his pale belly covered in coarse black hairs, and a pair of dusty blue jeans, one hole torn in the left knee.

In his left hand, he was astonished to find a rifle, an AR-15, which he found impossible to release from his grip. In his right hand, he found a cellular phone, which he also could not put down. Instead, he noticed that his thumb seemed to move of its own accord, scrolling and tapping the screen intermittently. A look at the screen revealed that it was continuously flipping through right wing media posts and comments, from the Fox News homepage, to the Parler app, various reddit sub-threads, and so on.

Greg couldn't rationalize his situation. The world seemed cast in a phosphorescent glow, with everything tilted toward the red end of the color spectrum. Casting his eyes upward, he realized a possible explanation. He was wearing a red hat, its bill protruding out from his forehead and reflecting its brightness down into his eyes. He tried to push the hat off his head with the cell phone hand, but it wouldn't budge. It was as though the hat had been glued to his skull.

What's happening to me? he wanted to say out loud, but all that came from his lips was, "Make America Great Again."

He groaned listlessly and rolled up into a sitting position. Through the window by his bed, he had a rectangular camera lens view of the outside world. It was raining. The air had a cold damp feel to it, with the daylight seeming the muted gray of aluminum siding. From here he could see the neighbor's election sign in the yard that he had left up since November. It read: BIDEN HARRIS 2020.

Fucking rain, Greg tried to say. Instead, he heard the words, "Fucking liberals."

It was as though there were two competing versions of himself riding on parallel lines of train track in his head, and yet only one was being physically manifested. He did not feel disturbed by this. There was a strange complacency sweeping through him. He knew that soon these competing railway lines would converge, and eventually he would forget all about his previous life. Though he could not remember how this came to pass (the last thing he remembered was watching an episode of Tucker Carlson and then going to a forum he liked in which people openly discussed the latest conspiracies), he was completely comfortable with the changes taking place in his mind and body.

His phone vibrated in his hand and a message came across from his sister. It read: Are you awake? Do you want some breakfast?

Instead of responding to the message, Greg decided to open the door of his room, which was quite difficult given the state his hands were in, and walk the short distance down the hallway to the kitchen. He carried the AR-15 in his left hand by its barrel grip, like a misbalanced club. There wasn't a lot of commotion coming from the kitchen, but he did hear some movement as he approached, letting him know it wasn't empty, and he could smell the welcoming aroma of bacon being fried. However, what he saw when he strode past the entryway of the dining area, was enough to drive any rational being to the point of madness.

Sitting at the dining table was a giant insect. It appeared to be a cockroach. Its body glistened slickly in the lights from overhead. Long antennae extended from its round black globe of a head and waggled clumsily over the polished surface of the wood. He could see four spiny arms clattering against the white plates and cutlery, making a quiet racket of indiscriminate noises, scrapes against glass and metal and wood. He noticed that obscenely, there were pancakes stacked on the plates, and syrup spilling over the plate edges, pooling on the table itself and spilling slowly toward the floor. Worse than the sight of it, was the smell. He could smell the sickly odor of the bug, a kind of acrid and noxious chemical scent that burned his sinuses.

As if this wasn't enough, he looked past the roach, and with horror draining the blood from his face, found that it wasn't alone. In the kitchen itself, standing near the stove, was a giant rat. The rat stood on its hind legs, its forelegs balancing it up on the counter, one bright pink paw holding the handle of a skillet. The rat looked like it had just crawled out of a wet gutter. Its fur was partially damp and matted with pieces of broken leaves. A thick rope of flesh that was its tail slithered and jerked near the floor like a sightless snake bristled with random growths of hair and cracked all over with wrinkles. The rat turned toward him and sneered, exposing its giant incisors, its black eyes glittering madly like polished and soulless orbs of insanity. A strand of drool dripped from its open mouth and sizzled when it hit the pan.

Greg wanted to scream, but found his throat too dry to allow speech. His hands seemed to act of their own accord again. The right magically was able to deposit his phone into the rear pocket of his jeans, and then latched itself immediately to the trigger grip of his rifle, which he raised to his shoulder as mechanically and practiced as a robot soldier. His finger found the trigger and felt its springiness comforting and cold.

Then, the insect and the rat tried to speak to him.

It appeared they were trying to communicate to him something, their voices garbled and broken with alien guttural sounds of indescribable indecipherableness. To Greg, the only thing he could make out was apparently a repeated word, both the rat and the roach hissing through their own inhuman vocal cords, "*maggots....maggots....maggots. Maggots....MAGgots..magGOTS...*"

They made like they wanted to move in his direction. The roach pushed back from the table, its chair skittering backward and toppling over behind it.

"*Maggots…..magGOTS…..maGGots……*" they chanted discordantly.

"NO!" Greg shouted, finally finding his voice. "Don't come near me!"

He took a shuffling step backward, and his foot bumped against something that wasn't there two seconds before. Glancing down sent another jolt of maddening hysteria through his body and mind. There was what appeared to be an oversized cricket encroaching upon his space. It's brown-shelled body swelled and receded with ratcheting gasps of air. The forks of its antennae moved sporadically near his pant leg, and one seemed to almost want to caress his calf. In one of its appendages, there appeared to be a cellphone.

Greg shrieked and kicked at the giant insect to get it away from him. It was pushed on its side and rolled against the hallway wall, its spiny hind legs working in a frenzy. When he looked back up, he found the the roach and the rat had used this opportunity to close the gap between them. Greg's instincts took over. He opened fire, shooting bursts of rounds into both giant creatures, sending sprays of black fluid and blood spattering.

Time suddenly felt stretched. The air felt hot and sticky, and full of the scent of burnt metal. Both the rat and the roach screamed inhuman screams and recoiled backward, their bodies jerking with the impacts of the bullets, and then collapsing into spasmodic and lifeless heaps on the tiled floor. Their limbs quivered with brain death.

The rifle reports were deafening in such an enclosed space, and Greg's ears felt stuffed full of cotton, beneath which his mind seemed pierced with the hot needle of a steady ringing that swelled into a high pitched: *eeeeeeeeeeeee*. To make matters worse, the smoke alarms in the kitchen began to sound, as the bacon in the pan on the stove scorched and billowed black-gray smoke, a small flame *floofing* to life there like a candle lit to the memory of the carnivore. It was a scene Greg not only felt, but *tasted*.

Greg drew breath and retreated gradually, backing his way to his room and shutting the door again. He turned and put his back to the door and slid downward, drawing the rifle to his chest, feeling as though he couldn't get enough air though he had barely taken twenty steps. His heart hammered painfully against his ribcage. He had no idea what the fuck was going on. The smoke alarms continued their assault on his senses, making it hard to think through their cacophonous *beeep-BEEEEP, beeep-BEEEEEP*. He smacked his head roughly against the wood grain of the door, trying to clear his thoughts.

His phone vibrated inexplicably in his back pocket. He wanted to ignore it, his eyes glancing furtively about the mess of his room. But then it vibrated again. And again. His right hand, acting nearly of its own volition, released the trigger grip of the firearm and retrieved his phone in one fluid motion. It lifted the device to his face, and clicked open the screen so he could view what was sending him notifications. Text messages were waiting for his acknowledgment. Again, from his sister.

"YOU KILLED MOM AND DAD!!!!!!!!" the first one read.

"MOTHERFUCKER!!!!!!!!!!!!"

"MOM AND DAD ARE DEAD BECAUSE OF YOU!!!! WTF IS WRONG WITH YOU??!!!"

"THE POLICE ARE COMING NOW. I HOPE THEY KILL YOU!!! BASTARD!!!!!!"

Greg read the messages with a dawning dismay. Slowly, he realized what had taken place. There was only one explanation. Q had gifted him the ability to see liberals in their true form. The conspiracies were all true. It saddened him somewhat that they had infiltrated his own family, but at the same time, it was the ultimate test of his patriotism. He was happy to do the work of Q, to help Trump save humanity from the liberal agenda. Smiling to himself, he sent a message back to his traitorous sister.

"All liberals are vermin scum. An infestation to be exterminated. I'm sorry you couldn't be saved."

The sound of sirens wailing filled the air, another instrument added to the symphony of chaos. Greg slid the phone back into his pocket and again held his rifle at the ready. He scooted his position over to the window, so he could see what was coming. The sirens grew louder as they neared. Across the street, the neighbors had exited their house to see what the fuss was about. Unsurprisingly, Greg noticed that his neighbors were now both giant millipedes. Their myriad legs gyrated and squirmed as their sectioned bodies tilted and twisted, surveying the street.

Greg looked around him and found an ammunition storage box he had purchased at a military surplus store. He pulled it to rest beside his knee, and clicked open the lid. It was filled with extra clips of ammo for his AR, already loaded and ready to go. It was as if he knew this day was approaching. And now it was here.

He pulled two clips from the box, set them on the bed. Sort of grimacing, sort of smiling, he used the barrel of the gun to break the glass of his bedroom window, and rested it on the lip of the sill. Just then two police cruisers sped into view and screeched to a halt, coming from opposite ends of the street. They fishtailed and came to a stop with their front tires in the yard. Greg could smell the smoke from their tires. Giant insects spilled from the doors and stood partially obscured behind them, readying for battle.

One of the insectoid officers raised a megaphone in its limbs. Greg saw a bright silver badge affixed to its carapace, and it gleamed in the muted sunlight of the day. From the megaphone came the words he knew he would hear: *"Maggots…..maggots…...maggots. Maggots….maggots…..maggOTS."*

More police cars were arriving by the second.

Greg smiled to himself. This was it. This was the war that was promised. Finally, the liberals were gong to pay for what they had done to his once great country.

With the ghost of a smile still touching his lips, Greg began to open fire.

Make America great again, he thought to himself, watching a cockroach police officer crumple to the ground. *Make America great again.*

Part Two

1984 IN 2020

~after George Orwell

We live in a surveillance state.
Where eyes stare from photographs,
following.
This is what we wanted.
We carry the microphones.
Stare into the screens.
We share our waking thoughts
so that they can be policed.

Freedom is an inconvenience.
An illusion.
Freedom is the dream
we speak of while we sleep.
They're rewriting history,
changing our memory,
revising the dictionary,
the very definition
of what freedom can be.

We agree to the terms of this torture,
the daily structure
of alarm clock and wage,
the exchange of time
for meaningless days,
a rationing of the will.
Where every friendship
hides a potential spy,
and every love is sedition.

I almost remember

the music drifting through leaves,
the colors flashing
through the feathers of wings,
before my eyes adjusted
to the dullness
of this alcoholic veil,
before I accepted the gray walls
of my isolation cell.

I'm so happy here,
I cannot tell a lie.

YOUR MOTHER HAS A BEAUTIFUL CUNT

~ *after Henry Miller*

I want the world to scratch itself to death,
where everybody's giving birth to something
they'd rather lock in the cellar than feed.
All the beds are crawling
and the table tops blink
like giant turtle eyes.

Anxiety thrives in the lampshades.
What if your mother was a Parisian whore,
harvesting fly eggs from her nipples
like coagulated milk,
and you knew that's how she nursed you?

The Parisian streets are a confluence of cunts.
If time is a cancer then love is a leper
asking for a French kiss in exchange
for a poem, and a poem is just a penis
erected from words.

My poems made me pregnant.
I walk around with my belly exposed
and distended,
burping with poetic indigestion,
all these stanzas squirming, kicking.

This collection will be the last collection,
the poetry to end all poetry,
a leviathan of sunsets, lilac blooms,
broken teeth and hearts the size of moons
all stitched together
like Frankenstein's cadaver,
hand out, begging for a companion.

Maybe all women are masochists.
I imagine your mother's cunt
still smelling like your delicate baby head,
her flower petals pushed wide
and welcoming as a fontanel
pressed inward by probing fingers
placing puzzle pieces in the brain.

I imagine your mother as a Jewess,
kissing the shrine between my legs
while asking my opinion
on the conflict with Palestine,
her mouth like strings of code
bolstering the strength of the Iron Dome,
while outside infant body parts
rain down from the sky.

Your mother tells me she loves me
then pickpockets my jeans,
leaving me penniless in my sleep.
The night's firmament writhes
like a swarming nest of rats,
asking me to consume more classics,
to get my stomach full of cellulose

and verbs, a false nourishment
that robs creative desire
like a syphilis of the soul,
leaving me starving for art,
an artist with nothing to say
except I'm sorry, I never meant
to let Henry Miller make me
into the apotheosis of obscenity.

WORD WHORED

~after William S. Burroughs,
for the Poetry Police

The American cemetery is nothing
but coffee and blood,
drug addicts and info addicts
pouring their mucus membranes
full of battery acid for kicks,
sick yellow ghosts
caught in balloons
and tubes tethered to the sun.

Veins crawling with neon spiders,
a fix that hums like tinnitus
or a refrigerator stuffed with Coca-Cola
running in a bomb shelter or
a basement below the street
where JFK showed the world his brain.

These are the bites that glow
and pulse like liquid light.
These are the spiny tendril fingers
pointy and barbed with ticklish poison.
This is the American Dream
self-siphoning a hole
of Kool-aid laced gasoline.

I am Jack B. Nimble.
I am Jack B. Quick, of the Quicken and Loan,
son of Sam and a mouth
spilling rancid Quaker oatmeal
resembling liquified brains
or the last will and testament
of JFK's cerebellum.

I watched the doctor
masturbate feverish
as a kid with the alcohol shakes,
his eyes spilling centipedes,
kerosene, and runny egg yolk,
yellow as his semen
shooting against the wall,
his cubicle now a grotesque collection
of samples and abstract art collage
smelling like a rotten mountain
of rat bodies piled like they could
reach the moon,
and I felt my cock get hard.

This poem is an orgasm
gone so decadent
all the assholes are quivering
between the cheeks of assholes
stifling their ecstatic screams
squirming like worms in their seats.
I am the planet, the cephalopod,
the machine that devours screams.
I'm filling your ears
with the mucus and secretion
and fetidly fragrant semen
of words too obscene to breathe.

This poem is a gang rape,
a conflagration of penile knives
pumping in and out of eye sockets
and rectal vaginas alike.
This poem is teeth clamping down
on a scrotum like a thin fleshy
raisin and ripping it free
of an elderly body, setting the sky
ablaze with steaming blood
and the fireworks of throats

hungry for flame.

This poem is stealing
the virginity of the Virgin Mary,
a forceful moan of wind
ripping through clitoral skin
and painting the caverns
of press-ironed slacks
with her holy ejaculate piss,
the canyon cubicle temples
blue-black and business gray,
pin-striped suit faces
upturned to welcome
the spray of her incandescent shit.

I am just the conduit.
I am the lightning rod
of erectile nerve sense,
a climax of cerebral cortex
gone incandescently wild
like St. Elmo's Fire, electricity
skipping stones across the heads
of a multitude of dicks,
the flagpoles encircling the globe
like the stations of the cross,
wishy washy as a gay priest
granting sacraments to the sinful
or the diseased.

Your reaction is the expected
elicitation of being incensed,
an emotional response most akin
to shitting a razor
while someone fingers your gash.
I am nothing
but a windmill for laughs.
I revel in your outrage

like a burn victim rolling in gas
and slathering myself
with the sewage of your horrified gasps.

I take your petition and I fuck it,
I fuck it and I beat it
and I fuck it some more,
until it begs for forgiveness
for ever wishing
this pain to live anywhere else
but inside us.

Not only is it beautiful,
this depravity must not be denied,
lest it grow like the concept
of hell burst open wide,
a guilt this body
was just never meant to hide
within the parabola
of its senses.

THE WEREWOLF DOES THE FOXTROT

~after Hermann Hesse

You either go home and hang yourself,
or you hang your shirt up,
knowing that suicide's allure
is a mirage, a silver bullet
slotted beneath its hammer, gleaming.

But it's not an escape hatch,
it's just a condemnation
to repeat the whole damned game.
It's the mistake of time
to believe you can outsmart the werewolf.

This self-seriousness avoids
the cosmic joke of it all,
The self is not the self,
but a conflagration of selves,
competing to hear the music.

This reality is not your home,
it is simply a way station,
a temporary dance hall,
a battlefield where both sides know
the war will never resolve.

You will always fear death,
even if you find yourself dancing
and drunk in the arms of a girl
whose eyes hold the light
of a billion cathedrals on fire.

You think you're an artist,
that you deserve to hear
your own thoughts recited

in classrooms, behind lecterns,
your messages heavy as mountains,

when Mozart died a pauper,
his liver swollen with wine,
and his body tossed in a pit
sprinkled with shovels of lime.
Who the fuck are you?

The great sea of written words
swallows your poems
and absorbs them, churns them
within its amorphous and deitous mass,
never bothering to request your name.

Don't be ashamed. Love waits
somewhere beyond the blood raw
promise of the razor. Let the wolf
learn to dance all the steps of all the days,
until one night it finds itself

smiling for no reason at all,
lost in the moment
of a sky gifting its kisses
like messages in bottles
from all the wolves who came before.

A View from Above

~after E. M. Forster

Half god, half ghost,
the creature becomes degenerate,
blind to a world
of beautiful things
breaking beneath the dirty moon.

It's a portentous poetry
to wage war
against the spring,
where fate and coincidence
thrive like hydrangeas

and violets losing their leaves
to linger upon the surface
of love's sacred lake
we all wish to bathe in,
and emerge from refreshed,

never choosing which debris
clings like wet paper
to the dimpled flesh.
The choices seem guided
much as the truth

is most generally misunderstood,
and is therefore the hardest to convey,
like counting the feathers
in every flock of birds
taking flight within the throat.

A VERBOSE LUNCHEON FOR THESPIANS

~after F. Scott Fitzgerald

The sun is an obsequious waiter
bringing endless servings
of sweat and squint
upon its golden platter, by the pool.

The stars don't live in the sky,
but on the ground,
among us, drinking liquid light
from champagne flutes.

They mingle in the promenade,
like flocks of loquacious swans
too supercilious
to get their feet wet or their feathers wet,

torpid and tongue tied,
floating on the surface
of their own aloof and drunken
camaraderie, that cacophony

of voices competing for air
among the susurrant crowd.
Someone's in love
with someone else's wife,

someone's floundering
in the lifeboat
of their own moribund solipsism,
or the excuse to commit a crime.

Even the gods have flaws, after all.
Beneath that Rodanesque facade
grins the face of a fraud,

empty as a cash vault

in some abandoned desert casino,
but his eyes, blue as bathwater,
his eyes say the sand tastes
like salt in your caviar mouth,

that trading places with him
is your only way out,
and you should be willing
to give up your raft for redemption.

I AM UNKILLABLE

~after Saul Bellow

1.
Everything is an accident.
My conception,
the scar below my left eye,
bumping into the love of my life
in the apparel section of Walmart
folding a pair of silk panties,
and feeling like an arrow
fired through the ribs
of the last American buffalo.

It's an accident I wasn't born
a buffalo, that instead of emerging
from that dark tunnel
into a brightness that erupted
like an exploding star,
waking in a time
where cowboys were paid
to pile bloody hides into mountains
while rotting carcasses
attracted flies in the fields,

I woke up here,
where every day is another kind
of mass shooting,
and yet, all the bullets ricochet
around my head,
criss-crossing into the shapes
of pentagrams and other glyphs
that hold no power of protection,

just more accidents in the cosmos,
different types of collisions

or near collisions,
where just the wind
of a passing chunk of debris
changes its target trajectory,
altering all foreseeable events
for all of future history.

2.
The dark shadows move with the breeze,
they brush against my spirit,
reminding me: I want, I want, I want.

I want to burn like the brightest colors
bursting from the roses
planted along the fence row.

I want to scream, I'll blow my brains out!
rather than admit my frailty,
that I've faded like the elbows in an old jacket.

I want to taste my grandmother's cooking
one more time, just one more time,
that corn, yellow glistening with butter,

beans freckled with pepper and fragrantly
steeped in a pot of ham hock,
and so many potatoes, more than any man

could ever rightly consume. God,
how I miss it. How I miss those Sundays
after my weekly indoctrination,

teaching me that the dead
are never truly dead,

but they'll never make you breakfast.

I want to learn every instrument,
to create music as easily as breath,
to have the ability to express myself

in a way that surpasses language,
whether I'm busking in a subway
or standing on the polished stage

of the opera house in Sydney,
I'm reaching out across all barriers,
touching that place without words

and saying, this is what it means,
this is what it means to be alive,
and if you want to know

what the dead are singing
from just beyond their graves,
remember this, this song that was you.

3.
My heart is like an unfinished church,
strengthened by grief
and unanswered prayers
I am a raincoat worn in the desert,

while nurturing a kinship
with every living thing.
The truth comes in blows
that turn the world into a drum,

my skin the surface, stretched
over that resonant hollow
emitting the thunder of hurt,

incessant as a night bird

calling for a mate that doesn't come.
You're either content to be,
or perpetually becoming,
in a constant state of renewal,

discovery, unfolding like a crumpled page
set to a flame.

4.
Death licks his postage stamps
and mails all his packages
to the center of the universe,
envelopes filled with dust and dirt,
that no one ever opens directly,
rather it's another hand
clasping weakly at the loose soil
to drop in on your grave.

In the meantime we wait,
convinced every rain drop
is somehow guided by the winds of fate,
and those arrows that keep missing
the heart by breadths
no wider than an inch,
keep emboldening our belief
that Death keeps his watch
from considerable distance,

when just the opposite is true.
He's always there, the whisperer,
chanting, *I want, I want, I want,*
barely disturbing the hairs
of the hidden inner ear,
convincing the body

of its own distraction,
to waltz fearless into the lion's den
and lay a hand flat on its tongue.

Nothing is an accident.
From the stars to the tiniest gnats
buzzing around the eyes,
change is as inevitable
as it is necessary,
so when the arrow finally hits true
to stop the gears of time,
become the roar of the beast
that would tear your throat out
rather than live its days
shackled to the totems
of false gods.

A Transmigration of Human Invention

~*after Mark Twain*

Magicians don't believe in magic,
but a writer must hold fast
to the miracles of speech.

If words were water
the world would surely drown
in the Holy Fountain of the mind.

If words were fire
no forest could survive
the whirlwind of spark and tongue.

History repeats and enslaves
the less fortunate wretch,
where words are wizards

and armor is a clattering
bone shrine of excess.
Humans are nothing more

than sweating insects,
and time is the greatest telemarketer.
The past is a filthy thing.

Nature abhors a vacuum cleaner,
while I adore my mouth
as the greatest of enchantments,

capable of inventing industries
from the ethereal,

an electric alacrity for teeth,

the first use of the firearm
putting the monarchy in the ground,
then using the telephone

to ring my future self
across many centuries reborn,
asking the truth of my predictions.

TOO MANY WINTERS

~after Edith Wharton

Lust gathers like pipe smoke,
building cobwebs in the eaves,
its ethereal strands stretched
between untouching hands.

The high-boned cheeks
of matrimony can break a man,
have him restless with blood,
too mean to sleep,

a warmth that reddens windows
like a sunset while outside's storms
pitch white tents in the hills,
a glistening fabric of cold

that no fire can hope to subdue
for long. Is it wrong
to hunger for the softness
of a thrilling new skin,

to let sensation cure malaise
like a suppurant medicine,
to see the dark form awaiting
below the hill, and plunge forward

undaunted, free.

THE GHOST OF TOM JOAD

~after John Steinbeck

I'm where there's nothing
left to lose, the epitome of hunger,
a million stomachs growling
like one throat
gargling the ocean.

I'm where dissonance retreats
into sonorous sibilance,
a unity of voice and mind,
a violence
of fingernails digging
bloody grooves in palms,
where beatings beget beatings.

I'm where mine meets *mine*,
where the handle of the pickaxe
shines its polished shine,
the rusted heads dropped
to dirt and dust
in favor of freer swings.

I'm where mother's milk
nurses the earth, dribbles down
the whiskered chins
of the starved and the sick,
men too desperate to ever feel shamed,
too tired to ever turn
a brother into a dollar.

I'm where dollars turn
into ashes inside mouths,
where buildings crumble
like ancient teeth

grinding themselves to smoke,
where the only sin is the sin you know,
and the only law is forgetting
everything you ever believed you owned.

A THESIS ON FATALISM

~*after Thomas Hardy*

The sky is a useful instrument
for cataloging desire,
giving each and every star
an identity unrequited.

Tonight, Cassiopeia could be
a lantern mistaken for the moon,
where tongues become
illegible maps of the mind,

or a visage of tarnished brass
seen through a window
of clouded Venetian glass,
more mirror than divination.

Whether love becomes
the meaty fist hammered
down upon the table
to quiet the raucous

thoughts of men,
or the plaintive bleating
of newborn lambs
first discovering their hunger,

it exists like a madrigal
hummed to drown a memory,
a tune heard on a pan flute
that seemed alive in the trees

and that taste of pine
the day you first saw her
standing among the chickens

slinging corn from her hands.

The Starving Artist

~ *after Knut Hamsun*

This body, my wretched bag of worms,
this mind, a shadow self
steeped in wing and wind and pocket lint.

These words are splinters in my mouth,
taste of raw garlic cloves,
my ideas like autumn

and its colorful carnival of transience.
I've been chewing my arm chair.
Hunger attacks me relentlessly,

a drunkenness that erodes
inhibition like a fever fanning the flame
of foolish abandon toward

something far worse,
something without a name
that thoughts fail to touch.

I invent gibberish and what it means,
while my own spit makes me sick.
Writing poems is like sucking

on a smooth, dirty stone,
staving off pain, a placebo
for food. I would sell my eyes

for a spoonful of sugar,
when not even the buttons
from my clothes

contain enough bone

or value beyond
the purpose of holding.

SOMA HOLIDAY

~after Aldous Huxley

I drink to my annihilation.
The silence of stretched expectancy,

science of solidarity,
released in the crimson twilight,

supine as a fallen dancer.
Supernatural, and alone,

an embryo gestating
within the mouth of a trumpet.

The rushing emptiness
of the night, a replicating cell.

I am not myself,
a pneumatic vessel for meat,

trapped in the sibilance
of such savage emotions,

a skeleton erected as a totem
to the triumph of human impermanence.

I apologize
for my imperfection,

the Shakespearean ignobility
of this natural body

received like an acid tablet
pressed to an unwilling tongue.

An open letter to Sir Osis of the Live R.

~after DFW

Addiction is the slow absolution,
a white flag
or a burning of the map,
a release from the guilt
of being alive.

Estates of worry
build themselves
like a definition of god,
a convexity meningioma,
interfacing with the dawn
in permutations of complications.

Addiction is a parabola,
a perfectly mirrored symmetry
within the chaos of decline,
convexity versus concavity
until it cancels itself out,
like a lung
inhaling pure fire.

Addiction is a whore
who calls herself Miss Diagnosis,
persona non grata
and femme fatale,
pseudonym of Madame Psychosis,
the mother still connected
umbilically to her stillborn,
until swallowed
by a cloud of ravenous flies.

Addiction is a kind of physics,
an algorithm that explains
yellow skin and scabs,
bloodshot eyes and lips
gone blue,
where exercise itself
feels like a suicide.

It's not a disease,
it's a dis-ease,
an entire universe alive
and humming
within the confines
of a tennis ball
thrown repeatedly
against the wall.

Ne te quaesiveris extra

~after Ralph Waldo Emerson

Seek no truth outside yourself,
all that matters is creation
listening to the heart's iron vibration.

Beware the bookworm
who smiles with tattered pages
stuck between teeth stained black with ink.

Nothing is original or unique,
even Shakespeare was known a thief,
a confluence of creative quills

and knives excising favorite lines.
A rose is perfection in repose,
and no writer can ever write a rose,

but nature is not a novelist.
Conformity is a conspiracy
to murder the mind, to murder God,

since God lives within the individual
divining inspiration from the flesh.
There is no escaping the self,

wherever you go is where you are
and imitation is suicide.
This poem is me killing myself.

Nothing is truly owned,
try holding the passing seconds
within your grasping hands,

so why aggregate inventive minds

into machinery's soulless hives?
By the time such clockwork gears

come grinding to a stop,
nothing alive will remember
how to reconstruct the heart.

SCHRODINGER'S PARADOXICAL ART

~after E. M. Cioran

At this moment I am
disappearing, even as your hands
hold words that were once
only thoughts in my ether,
now held as transient balloons
of creation within your consciousness
that you release
after but the briefest examination
back into that static cloud
of being and not being
minus any wool gathering eye,
I retract, or was I even here,
among the substratum,
the dust beneath the book,
beneath the bookshelf,
I remain free, free as a stillborn
or a miscarriage of language
without the burden of speech,
between the pyramids
and the morgue wavers
this illusion, this illusory self
incapable of connecting
with absence, a time before
this poem was written,
was printed upon pages
that soon yellowed
with the brittleness of age,
when everything itself
is just a breath
waiting to be perceived,
but by what, the salvation
of realizing salvation
is just the suicide of the future,

or the abortion of the poet
preventing the poem
from learning the fears
of the dying and the born.

A SCARY SCARY STORY

~after HG Wells

Behind a cheval glass,
I stand naked and cold,
a mirage of vacancy
silhouetted by snow.

Was that the wind
or some chattering teeth,
a chair that moves
and offers nothing a seat.

A skinless spirit
sits most at home
in an abandoned costume shop,
a ghost wears my clothes.

I am the invisible man!
I am the invisible man!
A body that houses
the whispers of the damned!

Those voices you hear,
the footsteps in the hall,
creaking hinges of doors
pushed open by none at all.

Is it imagination?
Or simply something more?
That shadow on the wall asking
if you thought to bolt the door.

THE SCAPEGOAT

~*after George Orwell*

Pigs don't have to fly
when they can walk
on two legs,
and teach the sheep to sing.

The windmill will never be finished.

All this work,
without the benefit of hands,
building the rainbow bridge
between now
and Sugar Candy Mountain.

Hear the raven
deliver his gospel,
the animalism
of instinct
pitted against intellect,
a kind of living revisionism.

This time, the windmill
will be as large as the world.

Snowball was no messiah,
he would have held
the whip in his teeth,
if he'd been given enough time
to blood his own slaves.

Everyone needs an enemy

in order to declare
victory

in this war, without invention,
peace is the windmill.

THE ROAD IS LIFE

~after Jack Kerouac

Roads and rivers and wild ribbons
of smoke trailing speeding locomotives
carrying travelers ever which way
like blood cells waving neck ties
long as telephone wires traversing
this crazy hill scape blurred by the passage
of inescapable time. The birds cry out,
their throats entire jazz bands
filling impossible crescendos
with white noise and black noise,
the music of life, the drum beat
of a billion stars pulsating
through the vacuum of the night,
saying witness me, love me, miss me
when I'm gone behind the veil
of another surreptitious summer,
warm sunshine and perfume,
where all the mad blossoms bloom
into the colors of their vestigial doom,
a fate that lingers behind all things,
an apparition of hands, moving mouths,
all faces swirling and blending into one,
this is it, man, this is the dream
the epiphany of a finger snapping
quick lightning through an inky fog,
brief illuminations of want
outlined in the milky violence
of a bruise the size of Texas
left on the shoulder of God.
It's sex. It's amphetamine. The first taste
of peaches and cream, and the wasted
bygone eras of a million broken strings,
broken chains, broken beams,

the rotted boards in the rotten porches
of the forgotten and empty swings,
all the houses crumbling across
the dusty and vacant plains,
where we once lived, where we once believed,
that all this was real, that it was tangible,
the smell, the touch, the flavor
of dust tinged rain quivering
the dry husks of the corn leaves,
and yes, we thought it would last forever.

PUNISHMENT

~ after Dostoevsky

Poverty, such a spiteful old widow,
and I, a beggar
beaten with a broom

fearful, frenzied, fantastic
embryo of an idea
within the eggshell of the mind

people are happier
with no need of locks,
shreds and scraps
of this reality

incongruous and enigmatic
the black snake
of wounded vanity

dressed to the nines
with half animate abortions,
caricatures of chess kings

distending its belly
with irregularities,
a requiem for the sanity
of suffering.

Capital. Just capital.
The false testimony
of the mad—

all men spill blood,
it flows like champagne
between the banks of the Neva.

The true crime of it all
is the suicide
of avoidance,

a Lazarus that rises
from the dead to the day
with no memory
of what came before.

THE PUNCHLINE OF THE JOKE

~after David Foster Wallace

Nothing is more important
than academia,
not God,
that infinite jester
whose real Bible
was the instruction booklet
to the first microwave oven
a meth addict used
to accidentally murder
their cat.

My PhD thesis
was a suicide note,
a detailed cryptographic duodenum
of perfunctory yet prodigious
self fellatio steeped in sadness,
but with an alcoholic heart,
like a list of philosophers' names
tattooed on a penile shaft,
how those names may shine
when smeared in saliva!
And oh, to see my own
among them, just before
that final bukakke breath.

The last poem I wrote
was supposed to be the LAST POEM
but then I discovered
the truth of my body,
and the joke of time,

of attempt, of will and restraint
and pleasure and faith
that falls like a gentle curtain
of detergent-sponsored rain.

Embrace this hedonism,
embrace this epiphany,
this self-fulfilling ejaculation,
that every body
is the same body,
and every mind
is just an expression
of that body,
wanting only to be held,
like the theory of an orchid
blooming but severed
from its nourishment's stem.

PRIME MERIDIAN

~after Cormac McCarthy

If time was a hammer
pounding the Earth flat
as the hardpan,
I could have been
the world's shittiest carpenter
but I've seen myself
as a homeless man
dragging a dog leash,
unable to let go
of that ghost
made from invisible flame.

Within fire lives
every fire and every man
burning
marionettes dangled from
the blind eye of the moon
beneath the turning wheel
of the firmament
ensconced with stars
and constellations traced wild
as a witch's signature

where God is war
a notion that's always been
and always will be,
awaiting its most dutiful supplicant,
soldiers
birthed from the ruinous dark
like a baby's lips shining

and spitting watermelon seeds,
Lincoln now the ferry man
floating the River Styx,
which is all rivers
their banks slaked with blood
between plains
battle fields, coffins, coffers.

We are taught stories
of hell beyond all reckoning,
but every smoke-filled breath
that burns the lungs
among the embers
scattered like incandescent chains
to the wind
is a hell of gunfire and thorns,
of want and possession,
and men with dirty hands
so caked with mud
their fingerprint whorls vanish
like inventions of ancestors
no one remembers the use of.

All this time, you've been afraid
to die, death like that
snaggle-toothed jackal
nipping at your heels.
But you just forgot
the bullet in your back
and the dream of yourself
you keep chasing
like the thin-legged shadow
of a coyote
dancing in the hills.

The Portrait of the Artist

~after Oscar Wilde

The artist has lost
the abstract sense of beauty,
thinking it more autobiography
than poetry, an excuse
to expose scars like a scaffold,
and then request applause.

Beauty is simply beauty
as sea is simply sea,
no allegory residing
within the sun or the sky.
A body is born,
and a body must die.

The artist cannot escape
the terror of his words.
A life wasted
trying to describe
the invisible mystery
of an oyster shell moon,

and the exact symphony
chorded by the wind
blowing through the illuminated
quivering blades of grass.
There is no music except
this silence, like a panegyric

composed and sang
by the cicada
sleeping beneath the soil.
To claim to know the purpose
of art's inner works

is like writing a love letter

to the memory of a corpse.
The artist lives forever,
a slave to the saturnine
cycles of the stage,
a wheel of hedonist rage
dripping the blood

of every experience possible
like illegible poems
upon the page. Art claims its space,
no matter the cost of wear
or guilt graying lines
in the stone statue museum

of the artist's face.
Time is the greatest liar,
just as it's the greatest thief,
which is why dust smells like childhood
and art seems to soothe
the weeping wounds of grief.

But, I ask you, after a thousand years,
who will still wonder
what any of this means?

THE PHYSICS OF THE GAME/THE BOMB

~after Don DeLillo

Two hundred sixteen raised red stitches
and the mathematics of disbelief,

warm peanuts in a brown paper sack
like individual Hail Marys waiting

to be shelled in that pause
between breath and the crack of the bat.

Look, I don't want to write another poem
about Death. But isn't every game

and every work of art just another attempt
at prolonging some sense of joy

in the chaotic lack of design,
like a scaffold built to harness the sun?

We take home our trophies with hope
of turning memories into heirlooms,

but the universal truth is a joke that falls flat
as a comedian puking on Frank Sinatra's shoes.

***

Perhaps all ghosts are holy,
sitting in the furrow of palpable destruction,
contrails in the skyline feathered and ribbed.

An architecture of nostalgia
connects the dots of the observable world,

the ripples and echoes of minute changes

unseen beneath the surface of what separates
this moment from what might have been,
the limb that snaps versus the limb that holds

under the dragging weight
of a tightening rope, a suicide or
a lynching gone horribly wrong, yet

extending the parameters of life's possible end.
After all, what really connects us to now,
other than a collective agreement

to acknowledge the other's existence,
to exhume the equivalent
of underground mountains

in order to store these actual mountains
of so much garbage, each item once its own
important and necessary creation

now just a placeholder signifying
10,000 years of decay, the same amount
of money it takes, to send your ashes to space.

****

I have an obdurate heart the heart of a raven pecking at the
eye of the crucified until I am the crucified an experience
outside of time that cheap and easy delusion that unifies
existence like the memory of where you were the morning of
9/11 or the day JFK died the moon landing the Challenger
explosion everything at once to the great nerve of the galaxy
where life is an illusory embellishment of thought gone wild
within the framework of its own beauty a geranium blooming

in the heart of Hiroshima or between the crack of concrete at the foot of the new Ground Zero where the subconscious is the perpetual backseat driver instinctual repetition to the point of boredom overlooking the answer to everything because it's always been so glaringly obvious so out in the open like condensation collecting on stained glass or statues erected in memoriam of tent pole extinctions and no not the Chicxulub Crater ha ha ha are you kidding singing 99 bottles of beer on the wall until you're back at the beginning with flashes of deja vu like glimpses of alternate lives flickering and spliced into the reels between birth and the opposite of birth but not death no never death

THE PERILS OF DISCOVERY

~after Joseph Conrad

Papier mache Mephistopheles
where the mangroves writhe
and darkness is an abeyance
of light struggling to survive,

we crawl through the throat
of the sleeping jungle snake
subcutaneously aware
of white eyes flaring wide

like temporary candles
lit and flaming, prayers for ivory
along the edges of the river.
What some would call savagery

I call the heart, the human condition,
a desire to see it through,
to sneak between the teeth
of the snapping gator's jaws,

lungs sputtering smoke
like a churning steamboat
beached in the muds of madness,
savage as a butcher's laughter,

you'll find me dancing
in the bloody pools of sacrifice
and cradling the shrunken heads
of the world's greatest philosophers.

GOD AND THE DEVIL LIVE IN KENTUCKY OR A PEDOPHILE'S PRAYER

~after William Faulkner

In the cold light
I live
hushed,
a shadow.

Where the shapes
move,
where the shapes
cry

like cold dark mouths
wet with dark,
wet with sound.
The light is a fire.

In the trees, I smell
the burning.
The leaves like sparks,
inverse moths.

I cry for the ground
to cover me,
absolve me
through soft earth,

now hard earth
absent of rain,
soft gray light
of a God damned sky.

The shapes move,
shadows upon shadows
kissing beasts
that open like hands,

open like mouths,
open like dark wounds
in the ground,
hushed and yearning

to be touched.
My hands soft fires
burning water
from the trees.

A LITTLE PATCH OF SKY

~after Marcel Proust

I wish I was a chrysanthemum,
kindled like an ephemeral star.

I wish I was a lilac tree,
blossoming purple and white.

I wish I was a trellis
of interwoven limbs, traced skyward,

fragrancing the blue, the ardor
for this approximate world.

I could be the taste, the texture,
orchid petal tongue,

dust clothed cowbell
dropped in petrichor, sea of green.

You could be my mother,
the pressed warmth of her bosom,

filling my mouth with salty milk,
saving me from Death.

You could be the cathedral
of cicada shell, of cellar smell,

an absence of senses
within my kaleidoscope dream.

I touch your hand, but I do not feel
your hand touching mine.

THE PALE FOUNTAIN

~after Vladimir Nabokov

It's difficult to nurse this
small, wild hope,
caught in the shadow of a waxwing,
indiscernible among the lacquered knitwork
of dark limbs and leaves
shivering like baby fingers along the wall,

this childish want
for poetry to live
as more than a didactic katydid
crying to be seen,
skulking and screaming to be
a recognized life amid the weeds
and myriad shades of green.

The tall clock keeps demolishing
the expectant wish
of immortality,
with every turn and click
of its mechanical guts
another possible future
retreats and crumbles to dust,
a poem unwriting itself
from the framework of never was.

There lies a hidden face
in the patterns unfolding
between a set of moth's wings,
a perfect camouflage
for resting on poplar bark
before approaching lights
like dilating stars in the dark,

and this could be a metaphor
for writing or for writers
chasing a dragon's tail
that in the ether gets lost
and forgotten to be attached,
part of their own body.

The writer exists forever
on the cusp of discovery,
lifting the thin, pale veil
between here and the imaginary,
a wanderer through smoke
in search of some fountain
and its cool waters
to touch and to drink,
then to lose and spend
the rest of these fluttering blinks
seeking to taste that bliss
again and again amen.

I pretend as you pretend
to be the caretaker
of my own thoughts,
and not just some character
pushed and pulled
like mail through invisible slots
and shipped toward destinations
governed by decisions
of alien robots, technology
whirring behind the scenes
of all creation, a microcosm
within a microcosm,
like a rose that blooms
infinitely inside itself,
and never knows
what color it is.

You Owe Me Your Heart

~after Truman Capote

It's better to look at the sky
than to live there, floating
before the fall,
an albatross
with no place to land.

Don't give your heart
to something wild,
the sea, or the wind,
the mare thrashing her neck
as she runs, treating all hands
like potential cages
meant for trapping birds.

She doesn't belong to you
because she's never accepted
a name, she's never felt
at home inside the glimmer
of light upon
a St. Christopher's medal.

Her home is somewhere south
of seconal and sunglasses,
of tigers and gin,
a place where bruises
have never kissed the flesh
of the apples,

and everything tastes
new and virginal,
the first burning malt
in a shot worth
one hundred years.

THE OFFENSIVE OR UNUSUAL NYMPHET

~after Vladimir Nabokov

Look at this tangle of thorns,
the sound of my infancy
a midge in the golden dusk.

The softness of baby animals,
an opalescent solipsism and pain
transcending tactile life.

A perversion of powerlessness,
a sculpture of loose panties
painted pink and pounded

from pig iron. I am weak.
I have only words
to play with. Something burning

that ought not to burn.
It's a pitiful tremor
that paws at me

like an adult cat
might batter about its prey,
adrenaline and fear

such a natural aphrodisiac
that tenderizes the meat
into succulent morsels.

Choose your favorite seduction,
says the pale spider

from its bed of soft spun silk,

each step forward cracking the mirror
of that expansive lake, frozen
into emerald ice, the color of vice.

Lust gathers like snow
on the apple-thin skin
of the world. Am I the apple,

or am I the world? Or maybe,
I am the virginal mouth,
strained, taut and stained with

candy red tartness.
A morbid allure
imprisons me

within its web
of laudanum-laced love.
A bad accident, bound

to happen soon,
a perfect murder of ballerinas
pirouetting beneath the water.

The price of such freedom
is the spider spinning
its own cocoon,

a reflection without its caster,
caught in that hourglass
hive of impure ideas humming.

MORTALITY IN THE TASTE OF AN APPLE

~after Gabriel Garcia Marquez

Blackbirds in the belfry,
bluebell blooms in the country fields,
eruptions of sound and color.

A cataclysm of dust,
cigarettes packed with ashes
cold as solitude.

Time is a circle
that encloses its passengers
within a straitjacket of cobwebs.

It's like keeping a scorpion
as a concubine,
expecting to die of natural causes.

Death is the most hospitable
of hosts, serving every meal
in its most flavorful form.

A moth made of gold
only flies in the vain,
all angels being virtuosos

of the harpsichord.
At the mercy of the wasps,
bedbugs eat the blood stains.

Have you ever seen an almond tree?
Rainwater gathers

in silver cisterns for cleansing feet.

Before the firing squad,
remember your laughter,
and the first kiss of the sea.

Our bodies are aging bananas,
taciturn chamber pots stacked and filled
with shit the same as diamonds.

A bric a brac world of red ants
and decapitated mannequins,
the enduring passion of love's destruction.

Life is a wheel of memories
placed in a basket and floated downstream,
a train of endless cars

accepting only the dead
as disenchanted inhabitants,
yellow butterflies that eat only ghosts.

A Marriage of Convenience

~after Jane Austen

When a woman is successful
she's never in want
of a husband.

Her nerves, like old friends,
hold an elegance
of misfortune.

What is marriage
but a contest of wills, a wager
who can outlive the other?

The societal frills
have blown ragged
as wedding veils

tied to cannibal crosses
like cancer ribbons,
yet teacups are still held

just so, pinky extended.
It's men
crying to be cut down now,

and one word
silences them forever —
empowerment.

When a woman is successful
she recites her vows

to the hammer,

prayer like flecks of glass
caught on her eyelashes,
her ring at the end of a chain

a reminder now of mothers
sipping tea as slaves,
wedded to counting the days.

MAN/MOUNTAIN/DUST MOTE

~after Jonathan Swift

Even the smallest of circles
contains 360 degrees,
from particles of molecular matter
to the expanding orb
of everything known,
the measurement can never change.

Consider time,
an enclosed loop
that neither begins nor ends
except from a stationary point
of limited perspective,
and itself a circle
spinning like a weathervane
inside the mind.

I reach out my hand
into the dust cloud
dancing like a nebula
within a slanted beam,
and I cause it to stir
like some plankton
before the mouth of a whale,

to this scattered fragmentation
of the past in decay,
I am the whale,
the whale the size of a mountain,
the mountain the size
of the sun.

Alien vessel, automaton
of observance,

island host
for microscopic lives
that live within lives, within lives,
walking across entire civilizations
building their cities underfoot,

together we wait
for either the scent of sulfur
or the taste of ash,
that moment of ignition
evaporating the sea
turning all thought
into pillars of senseless salt,
where everything
finally finds its liberty.

MAKING MAKE BELIEVE

~after Lewis Carroll

It's always six o'clock here, because it's always tea time,
just like I'm nowhere or everywhere, a Cheshire rhyme
juxtaposed without my emperor's new clothes
in a land of grass skies and blue sand between toes.

The rain falls up, where the clouds drink like cotton mouths
mumbling their thunder through stuttered broken vowels
without lightning or wind, a candy cane moon
pokes its nose between the scarlet begonia blooms,

saying hey, is this your dream, or are you in mine?
I can't remember myself or my most recent of crimes,
making me innocent until proven most utterly sane,
but with the things I've seen, can I really be blamed?

Sanity is subjective as are most of the arts,
put my head on a platter, give it to the Queen of Hearts.

THE MAGICIAN AND THE EVANGELICAL

~after Gabriel Garcia Marquez

The magnetism of gold
is a magnifying glass,
and science has eliminated
the concept of distance
between the Milky Way
and the rooftop.

Every person lives
as a fugitive from Death.

The alchemy of oranges
and mercurial devils
smelling sulfuric and secretive,
like a gypsy at night
coaxing love from the entrails
of cats, giving magic carpet rides.

The sea is all around us,
and yet we cannot find the sea.

Look at the begonias!
Look at the pendulum
that can lift any weight
other than itself!
These bones begin to fill
with the sounds of God!

When you've forgotten the names
of all known things, just point and nod.

Want suppurates and heals
the cracks in our broken shells,
an acolyte stands ringing
silver bells to ward off his hunger
while in the first graveyard
emaciated worms are singing.

Stopping desire is like eating dirt,
or a wedding cake made from the bark
of the withered chestnut trees.

Wrapped in a froth of needlework,
give the sacraments to the dying.
To touch ice for the first time
feels like a miracle, a levitation,
a flipping of the senses,
cold to hot and hot to cold.

Moderate the rigor of your mourning
and become a shroud of St. Elmo's Fire,

some place beyond vanity
where war is an emptiness without meaning—
it's always raining in August
and someone's immobile, asking for water.
What is the true location of the heart?
The chest, or the hidden home of nostalgia?

LIKE LIFE ITSELF

~after Leo Tolstoy

1.
Forget yourself and live
within the needs of time,
you know what you want to know,
that free will is an illusion,
so let the children play with pistols.

Life is like a quadrille
when you're waiting to dance
the mazurka, an unrequited
desire for sleep, the gaze
of a woman through a shop window,
mannequin in black velvet

unreachable

as a piebald mountain,
patches of snow
in the shapeless dark,
hazy cloudbank vapor veil
draped down the rock
like lace and tule
caressing a dancer's spine.

We live in the presence
of such mountains
we never intend to climb,
but the verdant contentedness
of the valley
can begin to feel morose,

and so.

A bohemian fire burns
hidden 'til quenched
within the familiarity of love,
the same the same the same,
music misunderstood,
a scattering of pearls
like misplaced faith
in medicine, no cure
for tuberculosis of the heart.

These fashionable gossips
seem antediluvian,
waiting for some angelic sword
to cleave through the fabric
of pleasurable disguise,
revealing life itself,
that yearning emptiness
beneath the floorboards of the world.

2.
Count every tree
like a funeral march,
the forest floor is a treble clef
and its music is the music
of crescendo and chaos,
of twig and stream and spring.
What is sound,
but the heartbeat of creation?

The best Russia
is the imaginary Russia
with its characters sculpted
from the clay of the page,

costumed in cravats, peacoats,
pock marks and rouge,
the crimson blush
of vodka cheeks and warmth
with a radiance like rage.

These secret lives,
secret thoughts, secret loves,
breathe beyond the magic
of selves intertwined
like the filigree vines of the Faberge.
Undress this sensuous arcade.

The eyes are fluent
in every language.

Yet, words fail the test
of emotional transcription,
robbing nature of its wonder,
trying to reduce beauty
through description, affix it
beneath glass and frame,
whittling the senses
with the dull edge
of a paper knife, pocket sized.

This, is not the essence of life,
to forget the fragrance
of fresh cut hay,
the hovering interplay of flight
between the gnat and the hawk
sharing the same twilight sky,
the rough heft
of the scythe in the hand,
fresh tangles of brush
crushing underfoot
and the cooling calm

of creation
reveals itself to their fluttering lens
and they leave us holding
yet another work of art
forever unfinished.

6.
O, Lord.
Death becomes boredom incarnate,
with all suffering burdens
sourced from the body,
the sufferings do their work,
shuffling the mind
more and more in preparation
for the great precipice
or river or chasm or void.

Is this body a windmill,
a being of blades,
of gale, of tower,
of rust and wood and nail,
a constant turning
of the wheel
transmigrating the dying
into the temples of the born?

Every woman eventually
becomes a mother,
even if only in the mind
of the motherless,
and every person is an orphan
who lives to see
those coffins lowered
into the tilled earth
filled and watered like
untenable seeds for grief.

You're either a widow
or a widow in waiting,
standing by a window
opaquely glazed with fog.

As beings, we orbit
into incomprehensible tangles
the small planets of yarn
we call our lives,
while the larger workers
behind the scenes,
either deity or determinist,
whisk their scissors and needles,
knitting fabrics we never see
to blanket the firmament
with the afghans of our decisions.

7.
A ghost light fringes the leaves
of the lime trees
bowed in subservience
to the moon.

The dusk is greeted
by the discordant cries
of the frogs, while within the weeds
and the brambles and the mugginess
of the marshland, countless feathered
fowls stay hidden and nestled
safe from the stomachs of men.

There may be fireflies,
there may be floating feathers
and lost smatterings of pollen
caught on the coattails of the wind,

occasional flourishes of wings
beating against the water,
along with mating calls
pinging the hillsides and the hillocks,
sounding like hauntings
of what could have been
without the invention of gunpowder
or fire.

Life exists,
a Russian nesting doll of breath.

8.
All this, what's it for?
It must be more
than to merely live
and yet, no answer presents itself.

Emotion is by nature
illiterate,
with all smiles
carrying a death-like rigidity.

In the end, happiness
is a morphine drip
of miscommunication.

The mountains do not speak.
The rivers do not speak.
The verdant valleys do not speak.
The roads, the store fronts,
the interchangeable faces of strangers
passing the windows of the train
do not speak.

A newborn curls its saffron-tinted hands

around the finger of a giant,
oblivious of the machinations
of its own survival,
dependent on this deity.

The truth of life remains

unreachable
as a self
actualized in self-reliance
and fulfilled with the joys
of labor for the sake of labor
and love for the sake of love.

Is mortality a nesting doll
of suffering, or the lost feathers
scattering from the grouse
in the wake of a shotgun blast,
a train station of incessant noise,
signaling through thunder
how every path is a beginning
and an ending
connected by the same
stretch of track,
those steel rails humming
and lain countless generations
before the tickets
were ever printed?

9.
Do not throw yourself
beneath the wheels of a train
to escape the unexplainable
cycle of work and rest
pulling the prayers
from the fallow fields

Epilogue

A dust cloud hangs like a benzedrine dream, a word, a shape the mouth makes to exist within the song of the night. For the final time I have spoken to the dead, I am the last coward on Earth, afraid of the multi-colored dark. The elixir of life is a chimera becoming a ghost of its own father. Charles Bukowski is dead, the shadow of a fence post, science of the heart. If I wanted to end the world, I'd become a poet, an eternal optimist. Polish thy armor and prepare to keep nothing at bay before the invention of barbed wire, the sea brings its destruction to my deathbed. Tell the fire not to burn, the biography of getting it wrong, during the running of the bulls. I've never been to Coney Island, except in mercurial madness. The sea is my asylum, and weather its interpreter, inspiration's vein in the sizzling sound like frost on a bristle cone, a surveillance state, scratching itself to death in the American cemetery of coffee and blood. Go home and hang yourself, half god, half degenerate. The sun is a server of accidental conceptions, a magician with no self esteem building cobwebs in the cathedral eaves, the epitome of hunger, a useful instrument for cataloging desire within a body or a bag of worms. I drink to my annihilation, my addiction, my slow absolution. All that matters is creation, even as I am disappearing behind a cheval glass, teaching the sheep to sing. Blurred by the passage of inescapable time, poverty is a widow of academia, a hammer in the abstract, mathematics of disbelief. Where the mangroves writhe in the cold light I wish I was a chrysanthemum, nursing a small, wild hope, watching the sky like a tangle of thorns in the belfry. A successful woman contains everything known at tea time, the magnetism of gold, the Milky Way, an obdurate heart, so forget yourself and live.

UNREMEMBERED DREAMS

~after Kahlil Gibran

So many seek the truth from the sea,
as if expecting a lantern
filled with rainwater
to somehow provide light
and the warmth of a flame,

but the sea, much like existence,
remains mysterious,
reflective
as the birthplace of stars.

A Prophet could rise
from the waves,
clad in raiments
of dripping tides,
and offer to speak the truth
about the nature of time,
but who would listen now?

These voices are but echoes,
like fluttering wings
made of sharpened knives.

They say love is the ocean
that whispers between all lands,
they say that tomorrow
is the mother of your children,
the bow and the arrow
fired into infinity's brow.

They say let every apple eaten
become the flesh of a human heart,
where every blade of grass
is recognized the same
as the pillars of a temple
lifting the structures of the sky.

They say the tools of progress
are forged in the furnaces of despair,
only the ocean is an innocent
in the tumult of the storm.

They say all these attempts
to control the outcomes of our lives
are like chasing sunsets
while trying to trace the shadows
into chalk outlines.

There is no escaping this pain,
to live is to martyr one's self
for the sound of the wind,
whilst unfolding into a rose.

They say that knowledge
is like blood spilled
from a vampire's vein,
and to drink is but to create
a greater thirst one can never sate.

They say life is not a riddle
to be solved
just as death is not the end
of questions.

What once was day
is now the silence of sleep,
and what comes next
is the fabric
woven from unremembered dreams.

The author extends his thanks to publications where some of these poems were originally published: *Terror House Magazine, Punk Noir Magazine, ImpSpired, The Dead Mule of Southern Literature, The Rusty Truck, Outcast Press, Slipstream Press, A Thin Slice of Anxiety, Misery Tourism, Expat Press.*

Extra special thanks to George Bilgere, Norman Minnick, and John Guzlowski, for their kind words. Thanks to my wife, my family, my friends, and to you, reader.

Jay Sizemore is an American poet.

He currently lives and works in Portland, Oregon.

Made in the USA
Columbia, SC
21 June 2023